Timely. Relevant. Compassionate. "The Poor With Me" captures the world of inner-city medicine, as told by a dedicated physician with a compassionate heart for his patients. Author, Phil Johnston, in the tradition of Atul Gawande, demystifies medical practice to a special segment of the population. Like Gawande, Johnston is a masterful storyteller. Immensely readable, this compilation of enchanting stories of some of Johnston's Broad Street Clinic patients provides the reader with humor and honesty. The vignettes illustrate the life sagas of real people living in poverty, meeting major challenges in obtaining health care. "The Poor With Me" fills a gaping hole in popular medical literature by describing the intersection between serving neglected people living poverty and the business of medical care. The book is relevant to all of us who ask the question "is there hope for the future of health care in the United States?" It is relevant for all of us.

Linda Lambert

Instructional Services Librarian

Taylor University

These primary health care vignettes, written in a thoughtful, sometimes humorous, often heart tugging manner and in the style of British veterinarian James Herriot, accentuate the stark reality that every health care condition is complicated by poverty. This is a story of a physician approaching his inner city patients with compassion, respect and dignity. Dr. Johnston has committed his career to the notion that health care in the inner city starts with treating each patient with caring hands and a loving heart.

The Poor With Me is great reading for anyone interested in learning more about the reality of the culture of poverty. You will enjoy it, but will be challenged to a greater understanding of the sameness and the differences of life in poverty. It should be required for all medical and social work students as well as everyone working in the community health center environment.

Dale Benson MD, FACPE

Retired. Former Community Health Center CEO, Hospital Vice President, and President of the American College of Physician Executives

This absorbing collection of real-life vignettes – funny, tragic, and illuminating – reflects Dr. Johnston's practice in an urban indigent population that lacks money, education, and social infrastructure to access desperately needed health care. You'll meet such colorful characters as a 63-year-old Roller Derby queen and a patient who drives to the clinic without using her clutch. Then your heart will be broken by patients such as Earl – destitute, homeless, and suffering from an untreated lung tumor and TB. During the journey, we get profound insights on the sociology of poverty and the lack of human options hidden within our society of plenty; along the way, Dr. Johnston also provides advocacy for the nationwide network of Community Health Centers and the primary care that is the backbone of our medical system. If (as the Bible states) the poor will always be with us, after reading this book you'll fervently hope that compassionate, wise, and committed physicians such as Dr. Johnston will also be with us at least as long.

Peyton G. Townes, Jr.

Health Care Consultant / Trainer

Former Assistant Director and Development Director – HealthNet Community Health Centers (Indianapolis, IN)

The poor are with us. With gentle compassion, poignant insight, and humor, Dr. Johnston allows us a glimpse into the lives and challenges of the inner city poor.

Patsy D. Needham, M.D., dermatologist

The POOR
WITH ME

REFLECTIONS ON A CAREER OF
HEALTHCARE IN THE INNER CITY

The POOR
WITH ME

PHILIP E. JOHNSTON, MD

TATE PUBLISHING
AND ENTERPRISES, LLC

Published by Tate Publishing & Enterprises, LLC
127 E. Trade Center Terrace | Mustang, Oklahoma 73064 USA
1.888.361.9473 | www.tatepublishing.com

Tate Publishing is committed to excellence in the publishing industry. The company reflects the philosophy established by the founders, based on Psalm 68:11,
"The Lord gave the word and great was the company of those who published it."

Book design copyright © 2014 by Tate Publishing, LLC. All rights reserved.
Cover design by Junriel Boquecosa
Interior design by Joana Quilantang

Published in the United States of America

ISBN: 978-1-63063-215-1
1. Biography & Autobiography / Medical
2. Medical / General
14.02.05

DEDICATION

To my mother Ruth, my wife Margaret, son Tim, and daughter Jen, the first sounding boards for these stories, I dedicate this written collection.

ACKNOWLEDGMENTS

Stories from a medical practice are influenced by countless individuals and the following chapters represent only a few of hundreds of stories that could be told. The patients who populate these chapters are merely a handful of tens of thousands with whom I have had the privilege to interact over forty years at the Broad Street Clinic. Those patients who have shown both loyalty and patience over these years are the ones who truly wrote this book. I am the scribe and have tremendous gratitude for what *they* have taught *me* over these four decades.

Over one hundred medical students, interns, and residents have spent one to three months on rotations with me, learning some of the nuances of "Community Medicine" in the inner city. Many of them have gone on to future practices in other specialties, but in their wake I have also benefitted as any teacher does from their contact. Among the dozens of colleagues and consultants with whom I have practiced over the years are many who have, like me, also borne the burden in the "heat" of inner city practice. They are too many to name.

But one individual deserves mention. Dr. Dale Benson is a fellow family physician whose gentle arm-twisting first convinced me of the value of inner city practice. His persistent vision, entrepreneurial skill, and administrative gifts were what brought the Broad Street Clinic and its now seven sister clinics to life and sustained them through many periods of "deep water". To all these diverse individuals, I owe a great debt of gratitude.

To my young friend, Munir Sayegh whose gifted pen and ink illustrations help bring the book and some of its vivid characters to life, I offer sincere thanks.

Finally, I must acknowledge the immense role that the Biblical pattern of Jesus has had both on my life and practice. He was the one who fulfilled the prophetic expectation to "preach good news to the *poor*" and spent much of his ministry life healing those with physical, emotional, and spiritual needs. The deep roots of my Christian faith and the model of Jesus' compassion for those around him in need have profoundly shaped my life and practice. To him belongs the greatest thanks!

TABLE OF CONTENTS

PREFACE

As a graduate physician finishes the long years of academic and clinical training, a decision about where to practice means answering a number of crucial questions. Do I join an existing practice or set out on my own? What environment do I want—urban, suburban, rural, academic? How can I generate enough income to pay off this huge school debt? The choice of specialty, made late in medical school to enter a residency, occurred months before, so the type of practice was predetermined.

When I finished my family practice residency in the early '70s, the specialty of family medicine was newly minted; residencies were competitive and often led by young, energetic physicians who were strongly committed to the values of their specialty. It was a high tide for primary care.

My decision to begin practice in an inner city neighborhood health center in a large mid-western city, designed to care for indigent poor patients, was not made lightly. My wife and I had two children and already had deep relationships in the area; I was familiar with the medical community since I'd trained there. The lure of a lucrative private practice was minimal, since my wife and I finished my medical school career debt free through frugal living. I felt a strong calling to care for disadvantaged populations. Also, the values we'd set early in our marriage to have our faith and family take highest priority in making decisions strongly influenced my choice of practice location.

The chapters that follow are the products of many years of fond reminiscences on that well-made decision and illustrate that inner city practice has unique challenges and rewards. There were innumerable patient interactions and clinical experiences that were the cause of chuckles, tears, frustrations, and considerable head scratching over what has now been an over forty year career in medical care. Many vignettes have faded into deserved obscurity. But the ones recorded here are authentic and completely factual, although all the names of people and places have been changed to respect confidentiality even though many of the patients are long gone.

Not all these stories have happy endings. But my hope is that in sharing these accounts, the reader will have a greater appreciation for the challenges of life and the medical problems faced by the people growing up in our inner cities. There may be a unique opportunity to compare this perspective with that which emerges after the promised Healthcare Reform. In the intervening interludes, I offer some observations about the effects of poverty on individuals, families, and communities regarding health care.

My desire is to simply share some of the humor as well as glimpses of wisdom that can be found within the wrenching drama that is a part of stressful everyday life in this unique segment of our American society.

INTRODUCTION

I was no exception to the general rule that physicians begin their practices with certain expectations regarding their patients' understanding of health care and partnership in their own care. Having grown up in a family with college educated parents, I was familiar with a culture in which it was common knowledge that not all infections required a shot or antibiotics, that immunizations were worthwhile and that some habits such as smoking and overeating were detrimental to health. Health education was a part of everyday life. Many patients in my inner city practice expected a "shot" for every cold but denied or were unaware of the dangers of a chronic but asymptomatic disease like hypertension. Was it true that a disturbing number of patients including diabetics *really* thought that a Coke and a bag of chips was a satisfactory breakfast?!

There were many formative experiences in my early years of practice at the Broad Street Clinic that helped me up the steep slope of the learning curve regarding the realities of an inner city practice with a rudimentary level of health education and the specter of financial disadvantage that governed indigent health care decisions. Very early, I learned that to be comprehensible, any written materials we used had to be geared to a third to fifth grade reading level. Since most commercially available health education materials were written for high school or above reading skills, we often had to compose our own brochures and handouts.

I could not take for granted that parents could reasonably discern the degree of urgency in calling after hours. It was more appropriate to affirm a worried mother calling about her two-year-old with vomiting, headache and a fever of one hundred three degrees than another calling because she was worried that her eight year old daughter had been exposed to head lice! It was a struggle to reassure a newly diagnosed fifty-year-old man that his new blood pressure medicine costing four dollars a month was affordable given that he was spending fifty dollars a month for cigarettes!

Two vignettes will be forever etched in my memory because they demonstrate both the health risks so typical for uninsured indigent patients rooted in the cost of care, and the sometimes dangerous hesitancy or overt barriers in obtaining urgently needed care dictated by the reality of living in destitution.

John Sullivan was one of my first patients. At fifty one, he and his wife had served as our clinic custodians since it opened. John was dutiful in taking his blood pressure medicines but had only a fifth grade education and his understanding of cardiac risk factors was minimal. He and his wife were proud that they owned their own house just down the alley from our clinic;

they lived simply and were proud of being debt free. Mr. Sullivan was stoic and had put up with increasing pain from his arthritic knees, no doubt aggravated by his work sweeping, mopping, climbing stairs. His most frequent question if I wanted to do a test or start new treatment was, "How much'll it cost"?

I was aghast one Monday morning when John was the first patient on my schedule because he'd been having "chest pain." When I saw him in the room, I knew he was in trouble. He related that he'd begun having chest pain two days before. He said it was like a vice on his chest; the pain went into his jaw. He was nauseated. He was pale. I took the time to do a quick EKG although I knew what the result would be. The tracing confirmed what I feared—John was having an acute myocardial infarction (heart attack) that had started forty eight hours before! His reluctance to get help was a direct result of the cost he knew would be associated with a hospitalization, hoping that it was "just heartburn" as he told me. In those days, (the early '70s) , John spent almost three weeks in the hospital and it was more than three months before he could come back to work. Could earlier intervention have helped? Absolutely! What was the barrier to care? A mix of naive underestimation of the severity of his symptoms along with the reality of the overwhelming cost of medical/hospital care combined to cost John far more than his meager income could afford.

Among my earliest patients, April Tharp was unique only because she was a member of a religious group that required her to keep evenings and weekends free to perform services. She had a low paying job as a motel maid, but was a meticulously faithful worker and, for a forty-three-year-old woman, had no chronic health problems. For many years, I'd followed an abnormal physical finding that she told me about on her first visit. After the birth of her third child ten years before, she'd had a breast infection while breast feeding that left her with two sizeable, hard lumps in her left breast. In the five years I'd been seeing her for annual exams, the lumps had remained unchanged and, with her urging and consent, I agreed to follow them without doing invasive testing. She'd had one mammogram that was "benign." Since she had no insurance, she was apprehensive about having further testing.

As time went on, the recommendations for following breast lumps became more stringent so that I finally urged her to have a diagnostic mammogram and consider having a biopsy. She reluctantly consented and we set up her appointment with a Breast Center. Several weeks later, I got a lab report documenting that April had gone through not only a mammogram, but an ultrasound, a needle biopsy and finally a lumpectomy—with a benign report: "calcified fibroadenoma." Then, for more than three years, I didn't see April at all.

She finally returned for an annual exam; although her breast exam was now normal, she had developed high blood pressure and required treatment with two drugs. As she told me her story, I was chagrinned that her only reason for waiting almost four years was that it took her that long on her maid salary to pay off the eight hundred dollar bill she'd incurred from her breast procedure. She was proud and frugal enough that she refused to consider going further in debt before she paid off the outstanding one.

Some of the stories that follow demonstrate aspects of this quandary: how does a health care provider give adequate and affordable medical care to patients who have both financial constraints and limited judgment about health priorities? How does one overcome a lifetime of inadequate basic health education and foster a new lifestyle of preventive care?

Of relevance in the current health care climate, how does promised Healthcare Reform intersect with both a growing need for primary care providers among disadvantaged populations and higher expectations and standards of care? Is it a losing battle or is there hope for the future of health care in the United States?

MRS. GRAY'S CLUTCH

Tuesdays often brought a risk for pedestrians along Broad Street near the clinic. That was the day when, once every month or two, Mrs. Lottie Gray started her ancient Dodge Dart and careened toward the clinic parking lot. Stories of her driving skills were legendary in the clinic neighborhood. Lottie had been a widow for over ten years and her husband had been a devotee of the manual transmission car. Unfortunately, he had apparently never felt the need to instruct his wife in the nuances of a clutch. My suspicion is that she saw that extra pedal next to the brake in her car as a strange nuisance, and her trajectory from her home several blocks north of the clinic supported that suspicion. I could usually hear her coming long before her arrival by the high pitched whine of the engine. I think she found second gear a convenient one to start in and simply revved the engine to whatever speed traffic would allow. The most dramatic part of her journey was the entry into the parking lot. Knowing Lottie was coming on Tuesdays, I rarely parked in the clinic lot, because she entered the lot at top speed, screeching around the corner and aiming in the general direction of the nearest open spot. Amazingly, she managed to avoid a grinding collision most of the time by braking to a stop, killing the engine without ever touching that mysterious clutch. Come to think of it, I never did look out to see how she managed to back up to get out of her space. It's probably good that remains a fascinating unknown.

On this particular Tuesday, Lottie expressed a truly unique chief complaint. The brief statement our medical assistants wrote in the chart to summarize the reason the patient needed medical attention: Mrs. Gray said she was "...being blown over by the wind"!

Lottie had always been a diminutive lady, another unnerving feature of watching her drive; on first glance, her car would appear to be driverless! But as I looked back in her chart, I saw that indeed she had been losing weight—from a high of about ninety-five pounds a year ago down to eighty-two—a disturbing trend in someone who was seventy-five years old. I also knew that Lottie was one of the common older ladies we had who were loathe to give up their clothes for an exam, so some of these weights might be falsely high. The winter before when she came in with influenza, I'd asked Lottie to "take off all your clothes from the waist up" and put on the gown I handed her. When I came back in the room, she'd dutifully taken off her sweater and blouse (but not slip or bra) and put her coat on *over* the gown! Since it was winter, but not really cold in the room, I chuckled and proceeded with the exam.

Today, as was often the case, nothing glaring showed up on her physical exam to explain a thirteen-pound weight loss; and a more thorough history didn't reveal any other likely suspects. In the week that followed, she brought in some stool samples to detect blood, and ominously, they were all positive. Since colon cancer was near the top of the list of prime suspects, and this was before the advent of colonoscopy, we arranged to have her get a barium enema, which was in those days the preferred diagnostic test to detect lower GI malignancy. The afternoon after she had the exam, I got a call from the attending radiologist. "Dr. Johnston? I'm afraid your patient, Mrs. Gray, has a tumor in her colon. It's down close to the cecum (near the appendix) and is almost certainly cancer." The good news was that he saw no suggestive signs that the tumor had penetrated or spread through the bowel wall, although there was no definitive way to tell about metastasis at that point.

I saw Mrs. Gray later that week and told her about the prospects. Although she didn't have insurance, she was anxious to be treated and knew that this meant surgery, probably to remove part of her colon with no assurance of a cure. Since I'd only finished my residency a couple years prior to this, one of my good friends was chief resident in the surgery program at our medical center. In those early days of inner city clinic practice, relationships with fellow residents and personal acquaintances with former staff physicians I'd trained with were my "safety valves" to get gratis help for the needy but uninsured patients. Thankfully, it was easy for my surgery resident friend to make an appointment for Lottie at the surgery clinic and to take her treatment the next step.

Some two weeks later after she'd had additional tests to be sure there was no evidence that the tumor had spread to other organs in her body, Lottie had her surgery. And again, I got a call from my friend and surgeon, Dr. Holmes when he finished. "Phil, I'm almost certain Lottie does have cancer. The tumor was the size of a soft ball and stuck to other loops of bowel. We did a resection but didn't have to do a colostomy. She'll be in the hospital several more days. I'll let you know when she's to be released and arrange for her to see an oncologist to decide when further cancer treatment should start." I saw Mrs. Gray in the hospital the next day and she had accepted the news remarkably well.

The following day when I stopped in to see her, Dr. Holmes was standing in the nurses' station holding her chart and reading a report with an incredulous smile on his face. "You're not going to believe this," he said and looked up. "Mrs. Gray doesn't have cancer after all! The pathologist said that tumor was from a chicken bone that got stuck in her appendix!" As we looked back on the sequence of events, it all fit. The weight loss, the blood in her stool, the abnormalities on her X-ray, even the appearance at surgery could be consistent with this diagnosis—extensive granulation tissue and scarring from a foreign body. Cancer was a far more common entity for these findings, but for Lottie, a misplaced chicken bone gave her a much more favorable outlook. Mrs. Gray received the news with amazing aplomb. "I knew God wouldn't desert me when this all happened. And, I'm still gonna eat chicken—just be more careful about bones!"

Some weeks later when Lottie returned to the clinic for a follow up, she had a big smile on her face when she said, "I'm not afraid of being out in the wind anymore!" And, she had gained five pounds, even with her coat off. When she left the room, she furtively squeezed a five dollar bill into my hand and said, "Thank you for helping me, Dr. Johnston. I'll never forget this, and I want this clinic to stay open!" My response was, "Mrs. Gray, with patients like you supporting us, we'll always be here to help"! But I don't think she ever figured out her clutch.

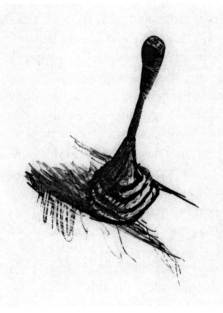

ANIMAL HAZARDS

Ordinarily, I don't consider a rooster a threatening animal. But that was before I met Mr. Fred Zolner. At the time he first came to see me, he was my oldest patient—a spry ninety-five-year-old, he lived by himself in the house he grew up in, an equally old and considerably more decrepit neighborhood landmark. His house was a small island, an ancient farm house on the fringes of inner city commercial sprawl. Before I even met Fred as a patient, I had stumbled on his house during one of my lunchtime walks, wondering who might live there in the midst of a roving menagerie of animals and a wild tangle of plants—part garden, part farm field, and part inner city weed patch. Mr. Zolner was a man of few words. I treated his arthritis and hypertension for several years with minimal complaints on his part. Laconic to a fault, he described his new presenting problem that day, as always, using generally three or four word sentences.

Fred: "My head hurts."

Me: "Why?"

Fred: "I got bit."

Me: "Bit? By what?"

Fred: "By my rooster!"

As the history progressed in the predictably jerky fashion, it turned out that among Fred's collection of animals was a rooster (never called by name) who literally ruled the roost. It wasn't enough for this rooster to merely protect his flock of a dozen hens, he aggressively threatened any interlopers; and Fred, as the official egg-gatherer, was seen as a genuine interloper. He was too slow to escape the rooster attack and suffered a significant gash in his sun-aged, mostly hairless scalp.

Although it didn't require suturing, it needed to be cleaned and dressed. In the process, I learned a bit more about Fred. He lost his wife in the distant past, had no children, and continued his rather Spartan life in a style reminiscent of the late nineteenth rather than the twentieth century. His health was remarkably good considering his age, and he seemed satisfied to live in the company of his many animals, some of which eventually supplemented his nutritional needs in addition to his abundant vegetable garden. On summer days, Fred was often found at the home-made stand in front of his house selling sweet corn, tomatoes, peppers, zucchini, and other typical mid-west garden produce. In a nostalgic way, he reminded me of my maternal grandfather whose cow, as we were growing up in a small, rural community in northern Indiana, was the source of all our milk and butter. Those early years included the memory of waking up to the distant chorus of roosters crowing. Even into his eighties, Grandpa would still tend his chickens in the barn behind his house in the town and then walk his lone Guernsey cow to the field behind our house on the edge of town. There they spent many hours in pastoral solitude. Mr. Zolner didn't have a cow; his chickens and the dominating rooster seemed to satisfy his need for companionship.

I saw him again, several months later for an unrelated problem. His scalp had healed perfectly and in curiosity I asked him. "How's that nasty rooster doing?"

To my surprise, he answered in a typically terse way, "He's daid!" Naturally, I was curious about the details, wondering if he'd finally been served for Sunday lunch. "How'd it happen?" I asked. After a moment, Fred responded dryly, "The goose pecked him to death!" It was one of Fred's longer sentences. "He's a mean critter, and I've never been able to ketch 'im." "What'll you do now?" I followed up. "I'll have him for Thanksgiving I s'pose," Fred answered. I don't remember seeing Fred again; I hope he wasn't the goose's last victim!

Mrs. Flossie Barton, unlike Fred, was neither a farmer nor the daughter of a farmer. She'd spent her whole life near down town and at the age of sixty-seven, seemed older than Fred. She'd struggled with diabetes most of her adult life and hadn't been able, even with concerted effort from our nutritionist and myself, to master the complexities of a diabetic diet. Her blood sugars were constantly over two-hundred and her weight exceeded that. She'd already had one knee replacement and needed to use a cane to get around safely; even with that assistance, her pace was glacial. I often had to help her into and out of the examination room simply to save time. Flossie's single passion was her cat, an ancient "Tom" of indeterminate age. However, he was decidedly short-tempered and demanding. She told me about the strict schedule he kept, demanding to be let out early each morning to explore the mysterious olfactory world that cats inhabit. However, Flossie's response time to feline demands became steadily more inadequate.

One morning, Flossie called our nurse saying that she'd been scratched by her cat and thought she needed to be seen. When I saw her that afternoon, I was aghast—the skin of both lower legs had been shredded! Although I knew something about Tom's reputation, I couldn't imagine how this had happened. I asked for clarification. Mrs. Barton's explanation was brief but illuminating. It appeared that the incident had occurred when Tom had requested an early exit from her house that morning, before she even got her bathrobe on. While opening the door, she'd lost her balance and without her cane to support her, accidentally stepped on Tom's tail. Significantly upset, Tom proceeded to let Flossie know about his displeasure by sharpening his claws on her legs. Alas, without the cane she was unable to respond quickly enough and spent a significant time extracting Tom's tail from under her slippered foot. Fortunately, the scratches, though numerous, were not deep; thorough cleaning, disinfecting, and dressing was sufficient. Still I did prescribe her an antibiotic and gave her a tetanus shot because of the amount of skin trauma she'd had and her less than optimal venous circulation. We also discussed where Tom's claws might have been in the preceding twenty-four hours.

Rarely did I consider a pet's actions a postoperative risk. Mrs. Mabel Ames proved me wrong. She was a dog lover and had adopted a large mixed breed from the humane society to keep her company after her husband died. They seemed to live in harmony: Mabel provided all his needs, and Rex provided her valuable companionship. Rex was also a formidable protector—merely hearing his warning bark was reportedly enough to scare off any potential intruder. His reputation was well known in the blocks around our clinic. Unfortunately, the neighboring dogs, in ways that only a canine mind can comprehend, were competing for dominance in the neighborhood and their fierce warning growls made walking Rex an aerobic event for Mabel.

Although hypertension was her most serious problem, Mabel's worsening vision problem proved to be a result of cataracts, a common diagnosis in an eighty-one-year-old patient. In the '70s, cataract surgery was not the elegant, quick, out-patient procedure it is now. There was a prescribed period of time after the operation when the patient was to avoid exertion that would raise their intra-ocular pressure during the healing period. Mrs. Ames was only a day post-op when the crisis happened. She'd called me after she'd been seen by her ophthalmologist, worried that she'd hurt her eye by straining too much. The eye surgeon had patched her eye again but told her he didn't think she'd done any damage. Curious about the story behind this, I asked what had led to the strain she described. "Well, it was Rex. We went for our first walk together after he'd stayed with my neighbors during surgery." I almost anticipated the rest of the story. Unfortunately, the neighbors were also owners of Rex's main dominance competitor in the area. There was an unanticipated meeting between the two dogs with the neighboring animal chained to his house and Rex on a choke chain. As she described it, the contest rapidly escalated to the point of being "...him or me." In straining to throttle Rex she felt pain in her eye and was worried that she'd done something terrible. By her description, Rex was briefly asphyxiated, requiring her to use mouth-to-muzzle resuscitation! Fortunately, her eye healed well and her blood pressure demonstrated no ill effects from her canine adventure.

Many inner city patients have few options or diversions. Life itself often demands all the energy and resources they can muster. Animals are usually a healthy respite. But, there are exceptions to every generality.

MATTIE CAN'T
REACH HER HAT

Not all of my patient contacts happened at the Broad Street Clinic. Our network now has eight clinics scattered through the inner city, and occasionally, I'd be asked to work at other sites. Much of the patient populations were similar, but there were some unique exceptions. Mattie Herman was one of the patients I saw several times at a different clinic. She had several of the vicissitudes of old age—a bit of arthritis and high blood pressure—but she was generally active and vivacious. She was a spry seventy-nine–year-old spinster who had two real passions in life.

First, she'd been a member for over sixty years of an inner city church that survived the suburban exodus. She had taught a Sunday school class of five-year-olds for years. Most of her former students had grown up and moved away, but some were still part of her church; she was universally called "Grandma Mattie". Second, Mattie also loved hats. She wore one every time she came to the clinic, but her particular obsession was her collection of "Sunday Hats" which, I found out later, were reserved only for Sunday. I had never seen one of those treasured hats. Although I only worked at that clinic once a week, it turned out that Mattie habitually showed up for her checkups on the Monday evenings I was there.

On one visit in early fall, I noticed a distinct change. Mattie didn't have her hat on! She didn't seem particularly upset about it, but when I asked her, she frowned and said, "For the last month or two, I've had a harder and harder time reaching my hats in the closet. Last week when I got up to go to church on Sunday morning, I simply could *not* reach the top shelf!" (Where she'd kept her Sunday hats was no longer a mystery.) "I was so embarrassed that I had to wear one of my everyday hats to church because they're stored lower! My shoulders are so sore I can't reach up any more, and my neck is getting too stiff to even *look* up! Can arthritis get worse that fast?" I did the usual exam to check her shoulders and neck: she could reach up and put her hands on top of her head, put her hands behind her back, her shoulder and neck range of motion was normal. When I commented about this, she declared, "It always seems to be worst first thing in the morning. I kind of limber up by afternoon and evening." She was already taking a low dose of an arthritis medicine, so we agreed that she'd try increasing the dose and do some shoulder and neck exercises for the next month.

In only three weeks, she came back with that mournful look on her face. "Dr. Johnston, it's gotten even worse. I can't even put my drinking glasses in the kitchen cupboard after breakfast anymore! I don't know what I'll do...." She was not anxious to see a specialist and had never been one to submit easily to blood tests. However, in those ensuing weeks, I'd begun to have this nagging suspicion that perhaps her weakness, shoulder pain, and morning stiffness might not be simply arthritis. A somewhat unusual condition called polymyalgia rheumatica (PMR) can present in exactly this way, abrupt onset, worse in the morning and almost always confined to patients over seventy. Although there are no definitive tests or X-rays to establish the diagnosis, one simple test is usually highly abnormal. It's called sedimentation rate, a general test for inflammation. We drew the blood sample, but I told Mattie I'd call her about the result since it was a Monday evening.

Two days later at the Broad Street Clinic, I got a call from another physician who worked full time at Mattie's clinic. "Hey, Phil, do you know Mattie Herman? I got a "panic value" back on her sed rate—it was 124! What's she got? Temporal arteritis?" Although this inflammatory condition also causes a high sed rate and often accompanies PMR, it also causes visual problems and tender arteries on the side of the head. Mattie had neither. "Nope," I said. "I'm pretty sure she's got just PMR. Do you have her phone number? I'll call her and get her on some meds." On the phone, it took a bit of time, but I explained to Mattie about her condition—that it was not arthritis, that it was almost certainly responsible for her symptoms, *and* that it had a very effective treatment. PMR is one of a small group of conditions that responds quickly and dramatically to prednisone, an oral steroid. Mattie was a bit apprehensive about taking a steroid but because I promised her that it should help very quickly if we were correct in the diagnosis, she consented to start the medicine. I called the prescription in to the pharmacy that Friday afternoon, hopeful that my predictions would be true.

When I went back to her clinic the following Monday evening, sure enough, Mattie was on the schedule. As I walked into the examination room, I could tell instantly what the response had been. Miss Herman had a huge smile on her face as she reached up and took off her hat, a magnificent *Sunday* hat! "Dr.

THE POOR WITH ME

Johnston," she said, "I could hardly believe it! When I got up to take that pill on Saturday morning, I was so stiff I could hardly brush my hair. But by that evening, I was feeling lots better. And by Sunday morning, the pain and stiffness were *gone*, praise the *Lord*!" She gave me a friendly squeeze on the arm as she left. "I think I'll start wearing a Sunday hat to all my clinic visits from now on!"

PARASITIC SURPRISES

Parasitology was a subject quickly forgotten after the fleeting exposure we had in medical school. Usually a brief interlude in otherwise interminable weeks of microbiology, it was focused on strange organisms that stealthily develop the ability to hitchhike along in or on the human body. Such things as protozoa, helminthes, nematodes, and cestodes are alien species, rarely seen in western medicine and rapidly forgotten after the required regurgitation on a scheduled test. I found parasites *fascinating*! Perhaps it was because of an early exposure to seeing lice on a grade school friend or hearing about amebiasis from visiting friends who lived and worked in developing countries. But the idea of a cryptic invader lurking inside the human body—its journey there often a bewildering maze of complexity—is intriguing.

A three month externship in South Africa had introduced me to the intricacies of malaria and schistosomiasis, but the reality of ascariasis was most memorable. Soon after we arrived at Mosvold Mission Hospital, I assisted in surgery to repair a devastating abdominal wound a young man had incurred in a machete fight. A long section of his bowel actually protruded out on his abdominal wall and an extensive repair, including a double barrel colostomy, was required. During the repair of numerous intestinal perforations at surgery, I was appalled to see large pale roundworms, six or eight inches long, wriggling out of the wounds, escaping into the surgical field. The missionary surgeon calmly picked them out and dropped them on the floor saying, "Oh those are just ascaris worms, everybody here has them!" Everything was a blur to me at that point and I pondered what it must be like to carry a collection of worms of that size around in your gut. The next morning as we made rounds, we came to the man whose abdominal injury we'd repaired the night before to find a Kafkaesque scene. Worms were "abandoning ship" and were escaping from every orifice and clogging his nasogastric tube. Again, staff nurses tended to it with perfect aplomb. He went on to recover uneventfully, and worm free at least for a time.

The garish specter of parasitology only occasionally reared its ugly head in our clinic practice. Now and then, we'd get an anguished, panic-stricken call from a young mother whose four–year-old had "just passed a snake". The memory of my medical school African externship returned in a flash. One of those stray ascarids brought in by a distressed mother made its home in a formalin bottle in my desk for many years, a graphic illustration for students of what "passing a snake" meant.

Much more intriguing was my experience with Ray Adams, a career truck driver who had been faithful in coming in every few months until his blood pressure was controlled enough to pass the requirement for his DOT license. Ray was a calm, matter-of-fact, and prototypical trucker, not prone to exaggeration, but also disinclined to come to the clinic for a trivial matter.

So it was with reasonable confidence that I treated him over the phone when he called saying he was passing little white worms. My experience had been that this complaint *always* meant pinworms, the most common intestinal parasite we saw, particularly in children. I prescribed the usual regimen of a single hundred milligram tablet of mebendazole.

Peculiarly, he called back several weeks later saying that he was "still passin' them little white worms!" In fact, he shared that his girlfriend was passing them too. Horizontal transmission of parasites is not unusual, so I suspected she was the reservoir from which he had been reinfected. This time, I treated them both simultaneously and repeated the dose in a week.

Within two weeks, he called again. "They're still here," he said, apologetically. "Well, Ray, you need to bring me a sample of what you're passing—it may not be pinworms after all," I suggested. A few days later, he brought in a sample of what was clearly *not* a pinworm. It was a small, pale, whitish, *rectangular* object, still expanding and contracting in dreadful parasitic fashion, outside its host. Although I'd never seen one, I suspected that this was, in fact, a tape worm segment! Not knowing what consultant to engage for such a problem, I called a pathologist on the faculty at the medical school. He told me to send it to him in a formalin preservative. Although he was familiar with the microanatomy of parasites, he had no clue about what the treatment was. Later that week, I received a letter saying that it was unequivocally a *Taenia saginata* proglottid, a segment from a beef tapeworm, commenting in genuinely dry, professorial fashion that, "…the preserved tapeworm segments had more than twelve lateral uterine segments after injecting with India ink and clearing with carbol-xylene". He added, "Please have your patient save his stool for a couple days after he's treated! We're always running out of material to demonstrate tape worms to our parasitology students."

After a bit of research, I discovered that I needed to treat Ray and his girlfriend with praziquantel, a medication specific for this parasite, but one I'd never prescribed before. As delicately as I could over the phone, I told him about the pathologist's request for him to save his stool samples after treatment. Although Ray promised he would, I half hoped he'd forget, certain that I was the one who'd have to *deliver* the specimen to the pathology department.

True to his word, Ray brought in his specimen, contained in a large shoe box enclosing a plastic bag. It had obviously been a prodigious accomplishment for him and his girlfriend. The whole thing was closed with duct tape and was sitting ominously on my desk when I arrived. It was spirited into an obscure refrigerator for the rest of the day. As evening came, I began to dread my delivery trip. It had been years since I'd been to University Hospital, and I was uncertain where the Pathology Department was. On arrival, I had the feeling of being a terrorist delivering a bomb—fearful of being discovered. "Can I help you?" The night watchman spoke far louder than seemed necessary. "Yes, I'm looking for the Pathology Department...Sir," I said. "Why do you need to go there *this time* of night," he asked, somewhat suspiciously now. "I need to deliver a sample," I responded hesitantly. "Can you come back tomorrow? They're closed now," was the firm retort. "But Dr. B., the pathologist, told me to bring this sample. It's for his students," I said more furtively, not wanting to be more explicit. "Oh well, in that case, I'll take you to his office." Fortunately, I'd prepared a note for such a contingency, explaining to Dr. B. what the encased shoebox held, and I was relieved to transfer the sample to its home on Dr. B's desk.

The next week, to my delight, I got a rhapsodic letter from Dr. B., thanking me effusively for the very adequate sample, which he predicted would be "...sufficient to teach about tape worms for the next decade." In the aftermath, Ray and his girlfriend recollected a time some months before when they'd shared another trucker friend's cookout of meat from a newly butchered steer which "was cooked pretty rare". They proved to be grateful patients, and I always regretted not crediting them to future medical students for their contribution to the fascinating world of study in parasitology.

QUEEN OF THE ROLLER RINK

Beginning each school year, there is a rush of adolescent patients who come into our clinic for Sports Physicals. High schools require students who are going to participate on their athletic teams to have a routine exam before they play. When I see Sports Physical as the chief complaint on a chart before the exam, not specifying which sport is involved, one of my favorite opening lines to break the ice with a hulking, two-hundred-forty-pound fifteen-year-old boy is to ask, "Hi, I guess you're here for your...Cheerleading physical?" That usually earns me the right to ask more important questions about the past year's academic record, and even plans for the future. But all these exams are to assure that their current state of health warrants playing sports.

Sue Akers was being seen for the opposite reason. She was a sixty-three-year-old semi-retired factory worker. She hadn't seen a doctor for over ten years but came in because she found herself increasingly *unable* to participate in her favorite sport. She had developed a lifelong skill in and love of roller skating. In the early to mid '70s, public roller skating rinks were still popular places for individuals and groups to spend a couple hours (often on weekend evenings) skating to popular tunes, which were either recorded or, in some popular establishments, live electronic organ music! There was a unique ambience there that became an addiction for Sue. Although I never saw her skate, from her story, she must have been quite adept. She could not only skate forwards and backwards but could also do jumps. However, a disturbing problem had begun over six months before her visit. Her endurance for vigorous skating was slowly being diminished by severe cramping in her left leg. At first, it would only happen after twenty to thirty minutes of skating; but as time went by, she could only skate for two or three minutes before she had to stop and rest her leg. The cramps became unbearable. She still worked three days a week but it was a sedentary job, and she only noticed the cramping if she walked for five to ten minutes or more.

Although she'd not seen a doctor for years, she thought she'd been in pretty good health. When I asked her about other issues, she admitted that her one and a half pack per day smoking habit was bad for her, but she felt she needed it to cope with the stresses of her family and work. Her main interest was to go back to skating! I had a student with me the day she came for her first exam, and I was gratified to have a patient to demonstrate so graphically what Sue's problem was. As we examined her legs, it was easy to see there was a difference in how they looked. Her left foot and lower leg were somewhat shiny but redder than her right when she sat on the examining table. When she lay down and we elevated her legs, the left one turned ominously pale. More importantly, the usual pulses that can be felt in a foot were absent in her left foot compared to the still somewhat weak ones on the right. Most tellingly, she had a distinct bruit—the sound like water rushing through a kinked hose—in her left groin. Before Mrs. Aker left the room or had any additional tests, we were able to tell her what was wrong. Her skating disability was because of hardening or blockage of the artery supplying her left leg. When she skated or walked too much, the muscles in her leg weren't getting enough blood supply to meet the needs for activity.

The next few weeks included a flurry of activities. First she had a study to determine just where and how severe the obstruction was. It turned out the blockage was fairly localized to a segment of the femoral artery high in her leg. Before the days of interventional angioplasty (stretching the artery open) or stenting (inserting a device to help keep it open), Sue faced the reality of needing an arterial bypass surgical procedure. Fortunately, she had no other signs of hardening of arteries elsewhere, particularly the heart, so she submitted to being scheduled for the required vascular surgery. Going from healthy-not-seeing-a-doctor-for-years to needing to have major surgery for Sue was a rude awakening, not uncommon for my clinic patients. She had reentered the health care system because of a life disrupting symptom and had to make some life-changing decisions. One of the most important was that when she entered the hospital for her surgery, she stopped smoking—permanently!

I wasn't involved in her surgery and didn't manage to see her in the hospital, but the surgeon's report was a positive one. He was able to bypass the clogged section of artery successfully and he commented that the "color of the leg post-operatively was normal," a good sign that sufficient circulation had been restored. The real test was yet to come, though. Unless she could return to her beloved skating rink at full speed, Sue would be disappointed.

Two or three months after her surgery, she returned for a checkup with me. When I walked in the room, she had that unmistakable big-smile sign of a therapeutic success. "Dr. Johnston," she said, "I'm skating again!" And, to cap it off, she continued, "I've already saved enough money by not smoking that I've bought myself a new pair of skates!"

A PROFOUND ARRHYTHMIA

Most fields of medicine have gone through dramatic transitions in the last forty years. Ways of diagnosis and options of therapy have negotiated unimaginable change. In no specialty has this been truer than in cardiology. In the late '60s, having a heart attack meant a week or more in the hospital with virtually no meaningful way to intervene; coronary artery by-pass surgery and acute treatment with clot-dissolving medicine, angioplasty, or stenting were still distant dreams. In the '70s, cardiac arrhythmias were treated with sometimes noxious drugs that could cause side effects almost as unpleasant as the rhythm disorder was dangerous.

David McMillan was one of my patients who had the misfortune of developing a cardiac problem that had a profound effect on his life—and mine. He was a stoic rotund machine operator whose twenty-five years of reliable work were interrupted by the onset of unpredictable fainting spells. A downward spiral of events followed. It didn't take long to identify the cause of his problem. David had a defect in his heart's rhythm system. Tests showed that he had these passing out spells when his heart went into an abnormal pattern of beating so fast that the circulation to his brain dropped and he lost consciousness. This diagnosis known as ventricular tachycardia is often associated with other kinds of heart disease and, in the mid-seventies, few medical treatments were effective.

The first blow to David was losing his job. Understandably, the combination of fainting spells and driving heavy equipment was not compatible. This reality in itself was devastating to him because with the job loss, an important part of his identity and pride in doing a job well dissolved. He was depressed at the prospect of not being able to support his wife and family well and faced the necessity of having to depend on outside agencies— food stamps and the dreaded specter of welfare—to get by. The medical help to treat his problem was distressingly ineffective. In spite of stronger and stronger medicines, his fainting spells continued. Controlling his arrhythmia often required stays in the hospital's cardiac care unit. He became a familiar inhabitant there. With the help of an aggressive cardiology fellow (advanced resident in cardiology), David was supplied with a then *investigational* drug, amiodarone, which at the time had to be imported from France because it was not yet available in the U.S. Although it did suppress most of David's spells, there was an unpleasant side effect: his skin slowly took on a dusky, silvery color. This added to his self-consciousness and distress and didn't restore what he most wanted—the independence and security of a respectable job.

Several months after I had last seen David in my clinic when he'd actually been pretty stable regarding his heart condition, I got a panic-stricken call from the hospital. The cardiology fellow was on the line. "Mr. McMillan just checked out of the hospital AMA (against medical advice)," he said nervously. "We'd had him here on a heart-monitored bed, and the nurse said he just pulled off his chest leads and left! The last rhythm we have recorded was V. tach (ventricular tachycardia)!" David had left the hospital in the midst of a heart irregularity that easily could have been lethal!

Later that week, Mr. McMillan appeared quite alive at our clinic. When I saw him, he had a somewhat sheepish look on his silvery face but was still stubbornly defiant about his behavior. I caught up on his condition and talked about the incident in the hospital. "Mr. McMillan, the heart doctor called me about your leaving the hospital," I remarked. "You surely know how serious your condition was at the time. You could have *died*! Whatever possessed you to leave the hospital under those circumstances?" His answer was brief, but as I have processed it over the years, was deeply profound. "I just got tired of people telling me what to do!"

As I imagined his perspective, I began to appreciate what it would be like to go into a food stamp office and be ordered, "Take this form, go over there and fill it out. Do you have your proof of income? Oh, this is your *first time* here? Well, you know you'll have to prove that you qualify...." The same scenario would be repeated many times over in other needed social service offices. And in the hospital, to be told, "No, Mr. McMillan, you cannot have that for lunch. It's got too much sodium in it." Or, "Yes, Mr. McMillan, we're going to have to try to cardiovert [1] you again. Yes, I know that's painful…" Or, even more demeaningly, "Can't you wait? We've got lots of other patients here, you know!" I've frequently told my students a variation of the old saying, "You can lead a horse to water,", and my ending was, "but until you've got him to float on his back, you haven't done much!" For David, being in a uniformly dependent role didn't come naturally. He chafed at the indignity of being in a hospital, especially when he didn't have the anchor of a job to come back to. In increasing measure since that time, I've learned from David's sage expression to be patient with those under my care who have had excessive advice about what to do.

Years later, I saw Mr. McMillan's wife, long after he had succumbed to his heart problems. I recounted this event to her for the first time. Tears came to her eyes as she said, "Yes, my husband was a stubborn man. But he always did what he thought was right, and he was good to us!"

MUSICAL INTERLUDES

Okay, I'll admit it. Music is my favorite avocation. In fact, if I thought I could make a living at it, I'd probably retire from medicine and follow Mr. Allen(see Mom in a Jar) into an ephemeral fantasy world of making music. Of course, having several close friends in the competitive real world of professional music is more than enough to jar me back into reality! My preferred musical environment would not be the popular Broad Street Clinic genre of country/western but of classical and choral music, as foreign to my patient population as listening to twelve-tone Chinese opera in Mandarin would be to me! Oddly, music has played a sometimes powerful role in patients' style and method of communication.

Alice Packer has been a many year patient at the Broad Street Clinic, with a fascinating mix of psychological and physical problems to deal with. An elusive cardiac arrhythmia kept me busy for many years until it finally revealed the telltale evidence of WPW syndrome [2]. Mixed with this was a series of crushing losses: marital breakup, loss of her only son when he was locked up for a major felony, recurrent job losses, and frustrated dreams of publishing a book of poetry. Beyond this, she was a talented artist often bringing us imaginative hand-drawn pictures of various staff members. And, on occasional Friday evenings, she would regale the patrons of a nearby Karaoke Bar (so I was told) with her own singing, accompanying herself with a guitar. At one visit, Alice gave me a surprise gift—a cassette tape of original music she had written and recorded herself. One or two numbers of her country/western style was about the limit of my tolerance at a single sitting, but as I listened to the tape over several days in my office, it dawned on me that Alice was singing me her psychological autobiography! They were all in the same key, but the proverbial successions of loss were all there—spouse, job, home, son, dreams of the future—the heart of country/western music provided her the perfect venue for communication.

Occasionally, a musical interlude would arise at a most unexpected moment. For many women, the annual pelvic exam and Pap smear is a stressful but still important aspect of preventive care for which creativity is vital to promote relaxation. It was not an entirely apocryphal medical school training program, in which male students were required during their rotation on OB/GYN, to anonymously undergo a sham "pelvic exam" by a similarly anonymous examiner to appreciate the view from the other end of the table. My medical assistants became very adept at quietly suggesting various techniques to help a patient relax prior to an exam such as counting the holes in the acoustical tile on the ceiling, among others. A young lady demonstrated a musical variation on this theme as she was being examined. I could tell by her posture of wide-eyed, hands-crossed-over-her-chest apprehension that she was uncomfortable. But as I sat down to start the exam, I had the uncontrollable urge to stand up again as she, quaveringly, began to whistle the National Anthem! We all relaxed as there was a short "salute" of laughter.

However, it was one of my many chronic schizophrenic patients who most vividly demonstrated the universal language of music. Rella Whitcomb was an endearing though difficult lady in her early fifties who had a number of chronic medical problems. Her psychiatric disorder, which had been treated since she was twenty-two, often requiring inpatient stays to stabilize psychotic thinking, was most dominant. I hadn't realized her hidden poetic gift until experiencing an event that poignantly illustrated the gratitude a patient can have for being offered empathetic care and a listening ear. The text that follows was actually part of a song Rella composed "for Dr. Johnston" while she was in the locked psych ward of the hospital. The scene is even more bizarre if you can picture the actual setting. Because she had flagrantly disobeyed the orders of the attending staff, Rella had been relegated to four-way restraints overnight. I was paying a courtesy call to check her medical problems when I arrived before seven o'clock that morning. Her room was dark. (It's hard to control the lights when you are in four-way restraints!) As I walked in, I heard Rella's raspy voice emanate eerily from the darkness. She was...*singing*! What follows is a partial text of the song she'd written in a letter she gave me later.

> Dr. Johnston is the Law. I don't know why we don't have more Dr.s like him. He's kept me straight all these years. When I'm scared, he takes away all my fears. He's my Dad now and I'm proud of him. But listen, he won't take no lip from me... Dr. Johnston made a special trip to see how I was doing. Boy, I felt like it was Christmas having him drop by.

I never did quite catch the tune, but it sounded vaguely like Home on the Range.

EVA'S BUZZER

Much as the presence of the Mental Health Center on our third floor was formative in my early years of inner city practice, the Senior Citizen Center on the second floor affected both my style of practice and nudged the age of our average patient firmly into the geriatric range. Many patients particularly utilized the Senior Citizen Center as a source of social contact with peers as their mobility diminished and families moved to the suburbs. The most popular attractions were the tables for billiards and pool as well as weekly bingo games. But by far the most utilized program was the daily hot lunch program. For two dollars, the seniors could gather and have a home-cooked meal, prepared by volunteer cooks right in their center. The menus were posted a week ahead of time and had predictable entrees but that is getting ahead of the story.

Among the cooks at the Senior Citizen Center were several of my Broad Street Clinic patients. One of the best known and endearing was Eva Braddock, a lady in her mid-seventies who was a fixture in the neighborhood. She'd grown up and lived her entire life near

Broad Street. Unfortunately, like many of that generation, she'd started smoking at a young age and had paid
the price by losing her larynx to cancer in her late sixties. She had tried to learn the technique of esophageal
speech [3] but had never mastered the technique. Thus,
Eva used a battery-powered buzzer placed over a spot
under her jaw and spoke using the buzzer's sound. The
result is a monotone but understandable vocalization.
Eva wore her buzzer in a holster around her waist and
was very adept at the technique. Eva was outgoing and
bubbly. Everyone was Eva's friend.

There were a number of unwritten rules for the seniors participating in the group activities. First, there was to be *no butting in line* for lunch. Even on the occasional days when time constraints made the senior offering my default lunch, I couldn't ignore the fierce glares from those seniors who had dutifully waited in line. I risked losing an arm if I cut in line! On the other hand, if I ventured into the senior citizen center after lunch on Thursday when they had the after dinner square dance, I could lose a leg by being sucked into the frenzied melee that drew everyone into participation!

Eva, however, was a stabilizing factor for everyone. Within a few visits, she would quickly learn everyone's favorite dishes. The second unwritten rule was that you could not criticize Eva's cooking. Only compliments were permitted. So it was that Eva learned about my unrequited love of sauerkraut. I'd grown up with that as a dietary staple in a home of Swiss/German heritage, but my wife did not share my occasional love of this ethnic delicacy. Every Wednesday, Eva served sauerkraut and wieners, an entrée the aroma of which dominated the Broad Street Clinic for hours after the lunchtime serving. Since it was only an occasional Wednesday that my schedule justified an actual visit to the senior lunch center, Eva had been so taken by my grateful reminiscences after the first couple of sauerkraut visits that she responded predictably.

Much to the olfactory dismay of my staff, Eva would dutifully bring a bowl of sauerkraut and wieners downstairs and place it on my office desk. Even though covered in aluminum foil, its fragrance rapidly filled the entire office area. It would announce its presence long before I returned to my desk after leaving the clinic for another lunch spot.

After at least a dozen such aromatic gifts on consecutive Wednesdays, my staff subtly reminded me that they had to eat their lunches in the lounge adjacent to my office and they would appreciate my telling Eva that her weekly gifts were appreciated but unnecessary. In subsequent Wednesdays, if I wanted my bowl of Eva's sauerkraut, I had to promise that I would make a personal visit to the second floor—respecting their gustatory rights. Eva buzzed me her understanding. As I recall, there was a minor payment involving a round or two of a square dance.

DERMATOLOGICAL CONUNDRUMS

The skin is the body's largest organ. Diseases that show up primarily with skin findings are as fascinating and diverse as they usually are objective. You can actually *see* what the patient has. Determining what the disease is often proves quite challenging. Although I sometimes tell my students jokingly, "There are only two kinds of skin diseases: things that are steroid sensitive and things that aren't," my dermatologist friends assure me (and my experiences have proved) that it's much more complicated than that! Things are often *not* what they appear to be!

Among the many skin conditions we see at the clinic, the allergic rash associated with poison ivy is somewhat seasonal but very common. Even though I spend much time dispensing with old wives tales about it, poison ivy dermatitis is usually easily recognizable and treatable. But the case of now anonymous twelve-year-old twin boys illustrates how challenging the diagnosis can be. I saw them early one summer after school was out. They presented with a worsening three or four day rash on their hands but most severely around their mouths. It was so bad that they could hardly eat or swallow. When I saw them, with their appropriately worried mother, they had a classic poison ivy rash on their hands—irregular red streaks and patches with occasional blistering. However, their mouths were appalling! The entire area around their mouths was red and puffy, their lips blistered and swollen almost beyond recognition. They could hardly talk because of the pain of moving their mouths. They'd only been able to drink through a straw for two days. They were miserable. When I asked them if they'd been playing outdoors around weeds or poison ivy, they admitted they'd been outside, but only confessed to playing baseball in a neighbor's yard. "But it looks like you'd been eating it! Did someone dare you to do something like that?" I said. They shook their head in unison, but I asked the mom because something looked a bit suspicious, "Has this ever happened before? What have they been playing with lately?" Their Mom assured me that they'd never had anything like this before, but then added, "They *have* made some blowguns they've been playing with in the basement. Their Dad had to take them away because they kept shooting their sister." The light began to dawn. "Have you been using those blowguns outdoors?" I asked the boys again. This time, there was a delayed but slow nod—*yes*—in unison. It turned out that they'd found some seeds that were just a perfect size for their blowguns and had been filling their mouths with the seeds to blow at neighbor targets. It soon became clear that they were poison ivy seeds. Although the poison ivy resin has little effect on the mucosal lining of the mouth and GI tract, it had played havoc with the skin around their mouths. Again, a course of steroids did wonders for their facial rash. Only their parents knew the outcome on the future of their blowguns.

Over years of experience in teaching students, I try to pass on common tips that are clues to a diagnosis. In the case of poison ivy dermatitis, I often found that little boys uniquely presented with a typical rash on their hands, arms, *and* on their genitals, because in the same exposure (running through weeds while playing outside) they'd find the need to urinate while the resin was still fresh on their unwashed hands. One instance that left me somewhat red-faced occurred on a day when I'd just shared this pearl of wisdom with a student. Minutes later, we saw a young boy whose chief complaint was listed as "Rash on hands and swelling of privates." As I pointed out the irony of timing, we confidently walked into the room to find a frightened four-year-old, and he had the classic poison ivy rash on his hands and arms. We asked the mother to help us examine his "privates," so she took his pants down as I waxed profoundly about the coincidence of this rash pattern. As we turned to look at his genitals, I was taken aback. He had absolutely *no* rash, but instead, his swelling was an inguinal hernia with a sizeable hydrocele (fluid in the scrotum). I looked up at the mom, somewhat embarrassed, and asked, "How long has he had this?" "Oh," she said, "that side's been swollen for about a year. Our other doctor told us it should probably be fixed, but this is the first time we've had insurance!"

Clarence Edgerton illustrates another aspect of the "It's not always what it appears to be" principle. Clarence was also a faithful patient. He'd actually been seen at a cardiology clinic because of congestive heart failure, but the cardiology fellow had referred him to a dermatologist because he complained of a growth on his back. The cardiologist could justifiably refer him without an exam since skin was out of his area of expertise. However, one of Clarence's biggest problems was that he had no money. Sometimes homeless, Mr. Edgerton was a typical clinic patient. He was often dependent on sample medicines to maintain his treatments. He certainly couldn't afford to pay for treatment of a cosmetic problem. Unfortunately, the dermatologist he saw was extremely busy and only examined him by looking down his shirt. "Oh, that's a seborrheic keratosis. I'd have to charge you ninety dollars to take that off, but you can see your clinic doctor for it." Dutifully, Clarence came in to see me for his keratosis. When I got a close look at it, the first clue that it wasn't the common seborrheic lesion was that—it moved! On inspection, I saw that it was an engorged tick about half an inch in breadth. Certainly from a distance, the grey color could have been mistaken for a seborrheic keratosis, but the treatment was much simpler, quicker and cheaper. Careful use of tweezers and a waste basket instead of a pathology report saved Clarence ninety dollars.

A RASH WITH RISKS

"Rash on arms for months" was the terse chief complaint on his chart. But my first glimpse of Max Moore made this complaint seem atypical. Usually, a 34-year-old man who is 6'2" and 340 lbs wouldn't be worried about a simple rash like this. My limited experience would have predicted that his visit might have been due to poison ivy, although the months of duration made that questionable. As I took his history, the usual suspects of working outdoors in weeds, changes in environmental exposure, or being around someone else with a similar rash were uniformly absent. Other aspects of his history were distressingly common: he'd had no medical care since his teenage years, smoked two packs of cigarettes a day for over twenty years, and admitted to drinking at least twelve beers on weekends.

As I plodded through Max's review of systems, I got some warning signals. He'd had increasing thirst (it was summer and he worked construction jobs). He had to get up at least twice a night to urinate and in spite of his current size, said he'd lost two inches in belt size in the last six months. Mr. Moore's family medical history was even more alarming. He acknowledged that his dad died at thirty-nine of a heart attack and a brother, now forty-three had also had a heart attack that he survived three years ago. After this revelation, a review of his personal history again suggested he had no chest pain, shortness of breath, or other warning signs of heart disease. I did his physical exam and found his blood pressure was 182/110. But the only other important physical finding other than his immense size was the rash he'd complained about: a scattering of scores of yellowish bumps of pinhead size over both arms.

I had seen eruptive xanthomas once or twice before, a rash that develops from very high levels of blood fats that closely resembled what I saw on Max. Clearly, he had a family history strongly suggestive there was a high probability that he had an inherited blood lipid (fat) problem, so I suggested that the cause of his rash might well be hyperlipidemia— high blood fats, cholesterol, and triglycerides particularly. "I don't care much what caused it, I just want this rash to go away. It's embarrassing and guys are teasing me about it," Max complained. He consented to come in for a fasting blood test.

Three or four days later when I got Max's blood work, I was astounded. He had the highest levels I'd ever seen— or even read about! His total cholesterol level was over six hundred (acceptable levels should be under two hundred), and his triglyceride level was over seven thousand! (Normal should be less than one hundred fifty). We'd also ordered a metabolic panel at the same time: his blood sugar was three hundred twenty.

Ever since that time, I've used Max as an unfortunate poster boy for cardiac risk factors. Of the major risk factors, he had them *all* except two: at age 34, he was still young and although at risk, had not as yet had a previous heart attack! He was a heavy smoker, obese, had high blood pressure, *and* diabetes—a frightening family history—and he was a *man*. The first time I saw him back after his blood tests, he remained unfazed. He was adamant that he wanted his rash to go away. Over the next few months, we bombarded Max with instructions (low fat, diabetic diet, weight loss guides) prescribed multiple medications to lower his blood pressure, sugar, and blood fat. Still, his concern was the same. "What about my rash?" His blood pressure remained 160/95 or higher, his weight *went up* to three hundred fifty, his sugar levels did come down, but only to about one hundred fifty in a fasting state at their lowest. In spite of diet and medications, his cholesterol stayed over three hundred and triglycerides were never under one thousand. He continued to smoke.

Then, for several months, Max Moore dropped off the radar screen. He didn't keep appointments, and we couldn't reach him by phone. The pharmacist said he wasn't picking up his medication refills. Finally, the day I dreaded came. Max had been admitted to the hospital for acute pancreatitis followed by surgery for a huge pseudocyst in his pancreas, all of which was probably a result of his high blood fats. The rash he hated was still there. I saw Max in the hospital a few times, but his care was being managed by an intensivist because he required parenteral feeding by a tube in a vein because his digestive system was being put at rest to help heal his pancreatic disease. This went on for over a month; Max chafed!

At last, I got a call from the hospital physician. He said that Max was to be put back on an oral diet the next day. Without planning it this way, I had a meeting early the next morning at the hospital. Max was out of his room getting tests done, so I wasn't able to see him, but as I walked out of the hospital toward the parking garage, a group of large people were walking in. I wasn't too surprised to see that it was Max's family coming to visit him. But it was with wry humor that I saw what they were carrying with them. It was a large bag from McDonalds, which the hospital physicians informed me later held a Big Mac and fries, the family's gift to Max the day he got off parenteral feedings!

Unfortunately, I was only rarely connected with Max after that. He was back in the hospital several times within the next two years for recurrent pancreatitis and his first heart attack eighteen months later. I honestly don't know what became of his rash. However, Max will forever be etched in my memory as the one patient who illustrated fully the reality of a "risky rash!"

COULD IT BE CANCER?

Although heart disease has been and still is the leading cause of death in the United States, regardless of financial status, cancer of all causes is next. The big three for women are breast, lung, and colorectal; although in inner city populations, lung cancer has long overtaken breast as the leading cause due to the high incidence of smoking. For men on the other hand, the leading deaths by cancer are from prostate, lung, and colorectal. All these diagnoses have been painfully common among my patients, but it is perhaps those more unusual forms of cancer that have proven to be the most intriguing.

It would be difficult to describe Rose Gibson with anything other than ordinary terms. Among my many clinic patients, she was as typical as any fifty-seven-year-old career waitress could be. In fact, she may well have been one of the many jeans-wearing, calls-you-honey women that made my lunches in the Broad Street neighborhood so homey. Rose's first visit was equally nondescript. She had the common triad of medical issues: high blood pressure, adult onset diabetes, and obesity. Within a few visits, these problems were controlled and less urgent preventive issues could be addressed. In fact, it was in follow up after her first (normal) mammogram that she mentioned the spot on her arm. "I think it's a place I burned myself years ago. In fact, another doctor took a piece of it to check it a few years ago and said it was okay," she claimed. I looked at the spot in question. It was on her right forearm and looked entirely benign. Measuring less than a quarter inch in diameter, symmetrically round in shape, slightly raised, and evenly colored, slightly paler than her skin, it looked like a simple skin polyp.

Rose presented a problem encountered with disturbing frequency among patients in poverty. She had no insurance, had just begun treatment with daily inexpensive medications for two newly diagnosed chronic diseases and had submitted to an uncomfortable preventative test. Should I now propose to her an expensive test (biopsy and histological evaluation) of what would almost certainly be a benign condition? Always in situations like this, an inner city doctor has to balance the patient's circumstance with clinical expertise and experience as well as the standard of care in the community. One of the axioms I learned from a wise dermatologist in my training was that "if something brings a skin lesion to a patient's attention, it deserves *your* attention and biopsy."

So, it was with some reluctance that I did a simple shave biopsy and sent the specimen to an out-of-state laboratory that was, at the time, our least expensive source of dermatological histopathology reporting. Then, for over a week, I waited; more accurately, I forgot about Rose's biopsy. After ten days, I now vividly remember the phone call—announced rather, as often was the case—with a droll audible page, "Dr. Johnston, call on line two. It's the lab." It was a Friday afternoon, a dreaded time to receive a call that required follow-up. As I picked up the phone, an unfamiliar voice said, "Dr. Johnston? This is Dr. Saiid and I have a report on Geepson, Ross. Do you have her chart?" At first, I couldn't understand his accent, and the name didn't ring a bell. "Geepson, Ross?" I responded. "What's the report about?" I queried, hoping for some more solid ground. "Eet's a skeen biopsy" came the reply. Immediately, I knew what it was about. No pathologist would make a personal call to the referring physician if it were only a skin polyp! But the next few words floored me. "Geepson, Ross has an amelanotic melanoma, and the melanoma cells go clear to the edge of the specimen. She will need a wide excision." "Thhanks", I stammered. "Will you send us a report?"

I had to call Rose with the news that afternoon. As is often typical of our patients, she took this bad news in stride. Her only question was, "What's next?" The next week brought the usual exercise of hoop-jumping: arranging a surgical consult through our county hospital and making all the arrangements for appointments, transportation, and follow up. Rose was a model of compliance even though it meant taking significant time away from her job. Fortunately, because of her twenty-five plus years of service, they were more lenient than many employers and were understanding of the requirement for time off. Within the next month, she had a wide excision of the skin around the original site of the melanoma and the required surgical exploration of the lymph nodes under her arm on that side. To her (and my) great relief, there were no signs of tumor spread in the lymph nodes, and the outlook was good.

As is too often the case, even that relatively minor procedure with significantly reduced fees by the county hospital left Rose with a two-thousand-dollar bill. Consequently, she came back only one time in the next three years as she faithfully tried to pay off her medical bills. She regularly took her daily diabetic and high blood pressure medicines, and still worked every day.

When she finally came back for a full visit three years later, she had a worried look on her face. "Doctor, I've got some swelling under my arm." My heart sank because it was the same arm her melanoma had been excised from. As I palpated her armpit, I dreaded what I felt: two vague lumps that ominously felt like lymph nodes. I checked the surgical scar where her surgery had been done and it looked perfect. But, as I did the rest of her exam, I was even more alarmed when I felt a small lump in her breast on the same side. When I showed Rose the area, I asked, "Have you felt this before?" "N-no. I've been afraid to check ever since I had that mammogram," she answered. A common fear among patients, I was chagrined that I hadn't been more firm in teaching her about this crucial part of self-care.

The next weeks included a succession of tests. Rose indeed had a tiny breast tumor that had already spread to the nodes in her armpit. In the months that followed there were surgeries, then chemotherapy and radiation.

Given the grim outlook if the sentinel nodes had been from a melanoma, Rose was better off with her breast tumor. She also finally qualified for state Medicaid and the tens of thousands of dollars in expenses were covered.

In the years that followed, I saw Rose regularly to adjust the treatment of her hypertension and diabetes as she remained under the care of an oncologist for her cancer. More than once during those years, Rose would express concern about a newly discovered lump or bump and would ask, "Can this be cancer?" After a careful exam, I would reassure her, "No, not this time, Rose. You've already had your share!"

CAUSES OF HEMOPTYSIS

Earl Horton was more than most a prototypical Broad Street Clinic patient. At age forty-eight, he had a colorful social and economic history, resulting in his being functionally homeless and, for most of the year, unemployed. However, Earl was fully employed each spring for a month. A large sports venue in our community holds a world class event attracting hundreds of thousands of enthusiasts; and the month following this event, scores of people find work cleaning up the detritus left by the departing fans. It's a time of great *plenty* for the Earls of our community, followed by eleven months of relative *want*. Earl was a sporadic visitor to the clinic, usually in the winter months of want when his lack of shelter often brought about virulent respiratory infections.

One unique aspect that marked Earl was his eyes. Years before, he had cataract surgery and in those days, implantable lenses weren't commonly used. The resulting corrective cataract lenses magnified his eyes enormously, giving him the appearance of a giant Cheshire Cat behind thick lenses. Additionally, he rarely cleaned his spectacles so that the first order of business when I saw him was to clean his classes so we could see each other. His personal hygiene also left much to be desired. Not having access to shower or laundry facilities most of the year resulted in a distinctive aroma following Earl like Charlie Brown's friend Pig-Pen was accompanied by a dust cloud.

I saw Earl near the end of a frigid February with complaints of fever and a severe cough. When I walked into the room, he was bundled in a heavy coat and still shaking from many hours in a brutal outdoor environment. As I helped him undress to be examined, he elaborated on his history. He'd been coughing for at least two months, and had seen blood in the mucous he coughed up in the last week or two. After removing his coat and at least three shirts, I came to the grimiest undershirt I'd ever seen. And as I tried to help him take that shirt off, it literally disintegrated, some of it sticking to his skin, other shards falling off and drifting to the floor like dirty snowflakes. His exam showed signs of pneumonia, and he'd lost over fifteen pounds since his last visit ten months before. Since tuberculosis was a top diagnostic possibility, we applied a TB skin test and sent him for a chest X-ray. Although the TB test was negative and his chest X-ray showed only mild pneumonia infiltrates and characteristics of chronic lung disease, I was still concerned that he might have TB and sent him finally to a pulmonologist.

A few days later, Dr. Kimmel called me after doing Earl's bronchoscopy. "Phil," he said, "Mr. Horton doesn't have TB. His bronchial washings were negative for acid fast bacilli. And, sorry to say, I found an endobronchial tumor that is probably the cause of his hemoptysis[4]. We don't have the pathology report back yet, but I bet it's a malignancy." Three days later, Dr. Kimmel's suspicions proved true, and Earl was scheduled for lung surgery. To our great surprise—and Earl's relief—the lung tumor was very small and localized. The surgeon was optimistic that he'd "got it all".

Later that spring, I saw Earl again and was grateful to see him looking well. "Earl," I said, "You've dodged a bullet this time! Let's make a plan for you to stop

smoking once and for all and find a place to stay permanently." Our social worker found a housing situation
that suited Earl's needs perfectly, and I was confident
that Earl was on an upward path.

Sadly, almost the same time the next winter, Earl
returned with an ominously familiar history. He had
spent his traditional spring month working, but with
the bonanza of income, he'd started smoking again,
had relapsed into his former drinking habits, and been
evicted from his housing. Of even more concern to me
was that he'd had another two-week bout of a respiratory infection, again accompanied by streaky hemoptysis. My immediate thought was naturally, *Sorry, Earl,
but I'm afraid Dr. Kimmel was wrong. This is almost certainly a recurrence of your lung cancer.* I didn't tell Earl
this, but I was virtually certain it would be the case.

I debated applying another TB test because I was
so sure his problem would be the same as before, so we
applied one and I sent him to see Dr. Kimmel again.
I got the expected call from Dr. Kimmel's office later
that week, but the report was entirely unexpected. After
finishing Earl's bronchoscopy, Dr. Kimmel reported,
"Well, I didn't see any tumor recurrence this time, but
he had lots of bronchial washings positive for acid fast
bacilli! And did you see his skin test? It's strongly positive! This time, it looks like Earl *does* have TB!"

For Earl, this was a new lease on life. He willingly
took his medications even though he knew it meant
daily doses for over a year. And, for the Broad Street
Clinic staff who had to be re-tested for TB (all were
negative) it seemed like a small price to pay. Six weeks

later when I saw Earl for his first follow-up, he looked great. "Doc, when you told me I'd dodged a bullet last year, I didn't realize the gun was still loaded! I'm gonna stop smoking for good; and my sister is taking me to AA meetings twice a week!" The real clue that Earl had turned over a new leaf was his glasses—they were already clean!

INTERLUDE I: POVERTY AND THE INDIVIDUAL

What is it that makes the Earl Hortons of our inner cities such a common fixture? Would Rose Gibson's story have been different if she had lived in an affluent suburb and had medical insurance? What issues in Max Moore's background (see A Rash With Risks) made his stormy and frustrating journey through various levels of health care so calamitous? All the stories included in this book are related by one common factor: they all are true-life sagas that illustrate the intersection between *individuals* living in poverty meeting major challenges in obtaining health care for diverse medical needs.

Social scientists have debated for years about the causes of inner city poverty. About the only thing that most agree on is that it is *complex* with no simple explanations or solutions. It didn't take many months of seeing patients at my inner city clinic to recognize some of the contributing factors. Mr. Horton, for instance—the man with a perplexing sequence of causes for coughing up blood—was a victim of a number of factors that trapped him in poverty. Social gurus like to talk about such things as *human capital*—the factors that enable a worker to be productive. As I grew up, I was part of a family that valued education, diligence in working (even earning fifty cents an hour helping a neighboring farmer work his fields when I was in junior high school!), and training that enabled me to gain new skills in being productive. The Mr. Hortons of our inner cities frequently lack the invaluable nurture of a parent or relative who encourages their education, rewards diligence, and models finding and keeping jobs that could lead to advancement and independence. Positive role models are often absent, and peers that share the same low expectations serve as negative influences. Among the relatively few individual patients who have escaped the inner city poverty climate they grew up in, virtually everyone I talked to could identify a person who took special interest in them—parent, grandparent, aunt/uncle, teacher, pastor—and mentored them in meaningful ways to shape their early experiences.

To be sure, the migration of jobs from the inner cities to the suburbs also contributes to the frequent joblessness or underemployment of men like Earl Horton. As well, the slow slide into despair and hopelessness about the future predictably gives rise to drinking and using other mind-altering substances to help cope with the daily realities that inner city residents find themselves in. These emotional issues and social habits also have a profound impact on the potential for an Earl Horton to gain the human capital, to escape the joblessness and homelessness that, in turn, has such a devastating effect on future health and health care.

There are benefit-less jobs, common among the Rose Gibsons of our inner cities who *do* work, but even those employers seldom provide insurance to cover health calamities like cancer. Immergence of a chronic disease such as diabetes or high blood pressure, which adds an increased burden to an already marginal family budget, proves disastrous. Social scientists talk about *structural economic shifts* to describe what has happened in our inner cities as jobs migrate to suburbs and a migration of people—often the skilled workers—accompanies or precedes this. Jobs that remain in the inner city tend to be low paying, low skill, and tedious ones that perpetuate the culture of poverty. Unfortunately, many of these inner city jobs pay just enough that workers cannot qualify for state or federal assistance through Medicaid or Medicare; a well-intentioned public policy to limit the breadth of coverage penalizes the faithful but low-paid workers in the inner city.

David McMillan (see A Profound Arrhythmia) worked at a low-paying job, which even provided rudimentary benefits, until he developed the cardiac arrhythmia that was his undoing. Frequent passing out spells weren't compatible with continued employment, and the discouraging slide into unintentional dependence made life miserable. There is a subtle social discrimination inherent in the inner city job market. Tolerance for absences, unexcused or even excused, is low and jobs are jeopardized; workers are replaced with little recourse. One aspect of inner city poverty that is not often written about, but which I see in the emotional desperation that is so common in Broad Street Clinic patients, is a result of a *lack of options*. When one steady source of income based on a sometimes menial skill is lost or a treasured past time has to be abandoned (such as Sue Akers' roller skating), few alternatives remain.

Many of these issues that affect individuals living in inner city poverty circumstances have a direct effect on both the providers of their health care and their health generally. Poverty can breed manipulative behavior. The pervasive lack of both necessities of life and the desirable things that are presented as normative by television and the media prompt subtle, or even overtly underhanded ways of illicit gain through medical care and care givers. Feigned medical conditions, purported disabilities, lost prescriptions become a pattern of interaction for individuals in chronic poverty situations. Distinguishing the real from the false becomes a challenge.

Providers can be overwhelmed by the magnitude of needs and the limited resources available to meet those needs. It is no wonder that our inner cities are frequently designated as medically underserved areas and few newly graduated primary care physicians are attracted to such a daunting practice environment unless it is to help pay off medical school loans. But medical communities are partnering to make care— even specialty care—more accessible. The Lottie Grays (see Mrs. Gray's Clutch) who patiently find their way through the maze of unfamiliar twists and turns in finding solutions to even unusual health problems demonstrate their gratitude in memorable ways. Perhaps the promise of Health Care Reform and the Affordable Health Care Act will encourage individuals troubled by inaccessible health care and make the prospect of finding that care more attractive.

MOM IN A JAR

The Allen family has been one that etched itself in my practice scrapbook as supremely memorable for a number of vaguely related reasons. My first contact was with the older daughter, Sherrill, proudly the first among the four Allen siblings to attain a paying job outside the home—as a nurse's aide. She was in her mid-thirties at the time and was indeed deserving of praise for escaping an odiously oppressive family situation. She was compulsively careful about her visits to the clinic, requiring a meticulously worded medical certificate signed by the doctor, justifying her absence from work. Her gratitude was shown by her bringing, on each visit, several usually outdated copies of often obscure medical journals (*Mycology Today*, *Gastroenterology for the Family Physician*, etc) that she had dutifully rescued from another physician's wastebasket to bring to me for my use. I was politely thankful.

Within six months of seeing Sherrill for the first time, I saw her younger brother, Thomas. In my contacts with him, his pervasive anxiety brought the dynamics of the Allen family into clearer focus. At age twenty-one, Tom had the indelible imprint of the effects of a father's endless criticism. His self-esteem was at low ebb, and he was constantly anxious and apprehensive about any attempt to achieve independence or self-sufficiency. Several efforts at school beyond high school ended in emotional crash and burns and retreating back to his home with mother, father, one brother and two sisters.

It was not until a year or more later that I met the father, Bruce Allen. Mr. Allen was a many year employee of a local industry and made sure that on his first visit to see me, I knew of his tenure of almost forty years there and his spotless attendance record. His medical problems were routine and didn't interfere with his work commitment. At sixty-five, he was near retirement and at his third or fourth visit, he began to share a dream for his post-retirement years. Thankfully, at that visit, I met his wife Janice Allen for the first time. It was in one of Bruce's early visits that he mentioned his love of Bluegrass music. He was part of a praise band at their inner city church, and this activity was one of the high points of Bruce's week. His dream, after retirement, was to form his own Bluegrass band and "tour churches down south". His wife was in the room when he shared this, and behind his back, I saw her roll her eyes. When he left the room to obtain a urine sample, she said, "Don't listen to him about this band! He's a terrible guitar player!" Bruce had a dream and expectations that were far beyond reality. Yet somehow, he had been able to stifle his children's expectations into oblivion. The mother, Janice, was a dutiful, submissive wife who tolerated her husband's eccentricities in spite of seeing the effect it had had on their children.

The youngest daughter, Emma, was the last of the Allen family for me to meet. Although above average intellectually and not unattractive, Emma was, early in her adult years, disabled by a cluster of functional complaints: chronic headaches, fibromyalgia, abdominal pain, and chronic fatigue. More than any of the other siblings, Emma illustrated the delicate balance between function and dysfunction that exists so often in many families trapped in the relentless many-faceted stresses of inner city life. Mr. Allen's iron-fisted disciplinary rule and his habitual criticism of the four children had a stultifying effect on their adolescent tasks of achieving independence. Social, psychological, and physical spin-offs had a devastating effect on the whole family.

Mrs. Allen had a common constellation of chronic medical problems. Fifteen years of diabetes and high blood pressure gradually took their toll on her vision and a stroke left her paralyzed on the right side and unable to speak at the age of seventy. Meanwhile, the domineering father, Bruce eased irascibly into retirement, never fully accepting the fading of the always illusive dream of becoming a touring Bluegrass performer. Slowly, his demeanor changed from being a strong, forceful, dominant influence in their household to being a distressingly forgetful curmudgeon. The progression of his Alzheimer's was even more distressing to the rest of the family as he rapidly became unable to care for himself and his deterioration led to the family placing him in a nursing home.

For four or five years following this, I cared for the rest of the family while Bruce was cared for by the nursing home physician. I got an occasional letter from the Allen siblings describing his slow decline but as the years went by, Bruce seemed to become mellower, going home for a visit every six months or so. Janice, however, declined rapidly and soon succumbed to the combined effects of diabetes and eventual renal failure after her stroke. Unwilling to break this news to Mr. Allen who remained in his Alzheimer Nursing Home Unit, the family mourned loss of their mother alone and decided on cremation rather than burial.

Several months after her mother's demise, I saw older sister Sherrill for an office visit. After dealing with her personal medical problems, I asked if she had any other questions. "Yes," she said, "I do. Dad's nursing home wants to let him come to see us again next week. But..." she paused, groping for the right words, "... mom's at home in a jar on the piano, and...what would we say?" It's the kind of question that even thirty five years of experience can't prepare a physician for. Since they hadn't yet told their father about his wife's passing, I told Sherrill that the family should probably take care of that first, perhaps with some of Mr. Allen's nursing home staff to help, then allow their father to grieve in whatever way seemed appropriate when he visited their home.

Three of the Allen siblings still live together in the homestead. Have I been able to teach them much or counteract the decades of dysfunctional home life? Can I claim any therapeutic triumphs or diagnostic break-throughs on behalf of the Allen family? It would be tempting to invoke diagnostic scapegoats like *chemical imbalance* or *obsessive-compulsive disorder* with over-tones of grandiosity. The sad fact is that I've probably learned far more from them than they have from me. Their survival as an intact, even though dysfunctional, family has been an illustrative example of the interplay between inner city life and the medical care challenges posed by such families.

WHAT ABOUT
THE WHITAKERS?

Although Mrs. Gray's reign of terror on the roads near my clinic was on occasional Tuesdays, year round, the Whitaker family presented a similar threat on Thursdays when their appointments tended to be. But their risk was seasonal. Mr. Whitaker only used his car on cold days in the fall and most of the winter when it was too cold or snowy to use the wheelbarrow. This may require some clarification. The Whitakers were a truly unique family. They lived only about five blocks from the clinic and if it were not for Mrs. Whitaker, they could have walked. Mrs. Whitaker was a reigning matriarch. She ruled the Whitaker family unequivocally. At fifty, she had an unusual combination of medical problems. She'd apparently inherited a rare syndrome[5] that caused her short stature (she was under five feet tall), round face, obesity, short arms and legs, and stubby fingers. As a result, Mrs. Whitaker couldn't walk more than a few steps—*forwards*. For some reason, (with a little help) she could walk the distance from our outside door to the examination rooms—*backwards*. On balmy days, Mr. Whitaker would trundle Mrs. Whitaker the five blocks to the clinic in his wheelbarrow. Then, he would patiently walk her, she shuffling backward, he in front of her going forward, down the halls to the examination room. It was a truly unique parade.

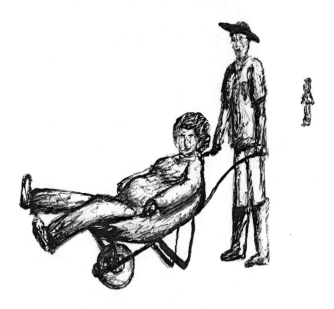

However, it was on winter days that the heart-stopping risk arose. Mr. Whitaker was legally blind. In actuality, he could see only a faint, blurred image ahead of him because he had a form of macular degeneration. However, for conflicting reasons to me, he still drove his car to transport the family to the clinic on the rare cold winter days when an appointment for one of the family was required. On at least two occasions, I was walking into the clinic when I saw the unmistakable Whitaker vehicle approaching. Mr. Whitaker was driving, but Mrs. Whitaker was sitting in the seat next to him, her short arms gesturing wildly, her head bobbing back and forth, and her mouth blurred as she jabbered directions. The car weaved back and forth, sometimes almost from curb to curb as they slowly approached the parking lot. Mr. Whitaker's peripheral vision was better than his central vision, so the corner was usually more successful than the Broad Street straight away. In the back seat of the car, or trailing behind the backward/forward procession of his parents into the clinic, was thirteen-year-old William Whitaker. The most frequent reason for clinic visits was Mrs. Whitaker's severe hypertension. Readings were often 220/130 or higher in spite of our best medication efforts. Unfortunately, Mrs. Whitaker found reasons *not* to take virtually any class of anti-hypertensive medicine we'd tried.

Both Mr. Whitaker and teenaged William were passive bystander/subjects to Mrs. Whitaker. She ordered them around—not only when they arrived in the clinic ("William, hold that door fer your father"; "Don't go so fast, Billy"; "We want the big room—this one's too small") but obviously at home as well. One sad afternoon, I received a phone call from CPS (Child Protective Services) that William was being taken out of the home. Apparently, neighbors had complained that in the evenings, they'd see William carrying buckets out to the storm drains. In the morning, they'd found human waste on the street near the drains and called the police. It turned out that the single commode in the Whitaker house had been defective for months and they were using the bathtub to collect waste. Mrs. Whitaker had given William the task of emptying the bathtub occasionally. CPS was asking me if I would testify at the court hearing to determine Mrs. Whitaker's competence as a mother.

Several months later, I was part of a theatrical hearing when a tearful Mrs. Whitaker expressed her apology for placing William in such a role and dramatically pled with the judge to allow William to stay with them since they had no other source of help as they were both *disabled*. William was returned to the home with careful restrictions put in place. A social worker visited them several times a week. The strange Whitaker procession continued for at least two more years with William remaining in the home, passive and silent at every visit and with Mrs. Whitaker's incredibly high blood pressures persisting. Finally, they disappeared, transferring their care to a hospital based clinic system more compatible with their needs.

About a year after they disappeared, I got a call from the coroner's office. The officer asked, "Do you know this Whitaker family down the street?" I said yes, but explained that we hadn't seen them for over a year. It turned out that the police had been called to the house again, this time summoned by Mrs. Whitaker herself. The coroner told me that the call was about an uncle who had moved from Tennessee to live with them a few weeks before. Nothing was known about the state of his health before, but when the police arrived, it appeared that Uncle Whitaker had ceased living at least two days before—sitting on the couch in the Whitaker's living room! When asked if they'd "noticed anything wrong with him," Mrs. Whitaker was heard to reply, "Well, yeh, he hain't been movin' much!"

I've often thought of this family, difficult to understand emotionally, challenging to treat medically, and tangled in complex social pathology. What could we have done to rescue little William? Whatever became of him as an adult? I don't know any of those answers. Again, the Whitakers represent an inner city family type trying to cope with normal activities of daily living but profoundly affected by difficult medical problems.

LAWRENCE WELK
COMES TO DINNER

The clinic where I began my practice was housed in what was once the Broad Street Methodist Church. Years before, the congregation had followed the migration of its congregation to the suburbs and sold their old building to the neighborhood association for one dollar. A local grant of several hundred thousand dollars helped create a passable medical space with eight examination rooms. Soon afterward, a Senior Citizen's Center became the flagship program of a Multiservice Center on the second floor and a Community Mental Health center occupied space on the third floor. It was in relationship to this third floor clinic that my appreciation of the emotionally debilitating disease of schizophrenia was broadened.

A chronic disease that affects its victim's perception of reality, schizophrenia often appears with disturbing symptoms in late adolescence and early adulthood. Pervasive delusions, disordered thinking, frightening auditory, and visual hallucinations are among the spectrum of findings that drastically interfere with every-day life. Prior to the discovery of effective treatments in the '50s, these were the patients that filled our asy-lums. As more and more therapeutic options became available, many patients with schizophrenia were able to maintain function within the context of community and family support. Yet, many of these patients still required regular therapy with both drugs and coun-seling—a role that community mental health centers filled admirably, particularly as space for long-term institutional psychiatric care dwindled. Because these mental health patients also developed more traditional medical problems, my relationship with the third floor was an intimate one. There was a time when I thought that twenty-five percent of my patient population was schizophrenic rather than the national incidence of one percent. Because there were so many of these patients needing medical care, the sometimes amusing interac-tions we had became legendary.

Very early in my days of taking medical histories, I went out of my way to use simple terms and understand-able language with any patient, particularly those with a disease that altered the perception of reality. Florence was such a new patient who, as I looked at the list of medicines she was already taking, was certainly schizo-phrenic because of being on an injectable anti-psychotic medication. As I began the history of her mental health problem, I politely asked, "How long have you had your 'nerve problem', Florence?" She immediately responded with a bright smile, "Oh, Doctor. I don't have a 'nerve problem.' I'm schizophrenic!" Florence helped me to address the problem more openly and explicitly!

Although not always characteristic of schizophrenia, *concrete thinking*—a diminished ability to abstract—occasionally prompted me to rethink my history taking. When I saw another new patient, a man in his seventies who was schizophrenic, I was examining his mouth for the first time. He'd clearly had a full mouth extraction, natural or assisted, many years before. Wondering about his ability to eat with no teeth, I asked while looking at his toothless mouth, "Do you have dentures?" Without hesitation, he replied "No, those are gums!"

Among many letters I've saved over the years are several from schizophrenic patients, distressed about their care, written from long-term psychiatric care facilities. Many are predictably incoherent but I saved them to demonstrate to students the realities of paranoia, tangential thinking, fixations, and *flights of ideas*, which are hallmarks of the thought disorders characteristic of these patients. Universally, they expressed appreciation for being heard and for a sympathetic, nonjudgmental acknowledgment of their disease. Among the letters was this one, quoted in part, retaining some of the original spelling and grammar that demonstrated as vividly as any text book, these unmistakable traits. Writing from the State Mental Institution, addressed to "Dr. Johnston, Broad Street Clinic, Examination room #4 (probably the last one I saw her in)

Dear Doktor,

I love you can you help me. I've been poisoned several times in here also I am doing so much better since I called the Prayer Line. M.S. is a communist but I know I am a missionary. Doktor, there is a raw gas leak in my room. I want to come home to you. The food is terrible. I know too much about the military they have me AWOL because I was saluting the flag. I was ready to go to church with my pastor but the Lord said go to McDonalds. HELP.

Love, R

Scattered through the sadly disjointed paragraph were apt illustrations of the propensity for fixations on religious and political agendas.

Two of my most endearing schizoid patients were a mother and daughter, Ava and Emily Barnes who, at ages eighty-one and fifty-three lived together, sharing the peculiarities of their schizophrenic illnesses. Although they were stable on their medications, they had a few recurring medical needs. For reasons that I never discovered, schizophrenia also seems to be associated with excessive toenail growth. Ava and Emily, at any rate, came in regularly every three months for my podiatric care. They were both of such girth that they were unable to muster the strength and dexterity needed to trim their huge nails. Nail trimming was a somewhat fulfilling diversion for me, but even with a pair of stout nail trimmers, the actual trimming was a hazardous occupation. My medical assistants soon learned to leave the room after dropping off the trimmers, fearful of being injured by a piece of nail that commonly ricocheted off the walls or ceiling in the heat of the battle.

I learned to be more cautious myself after an incident that brought my family into the fray. I'd seen Ava and Emily for their respective trims early in the morning and drove home after finishing clinic hours to a fond hug from my wife. But she then pushed away and stared up at my head. "What's that in your hair!" she asked apprehensively. I actually had hair sufficient for this to happen then, but as I brushed my hand over my head, a sizeable chunk of Barnes' toenail fell to the floor. In reflecting on the day, I wondered if anyone else had looked at my head closely enough to have detected what my wife saw instantly!

But the most fascinating aspect of Ava and Emily's history transpired during an off-handed conversation we had as they were leaving the examination room after a visit. Mother Ava was in the lead and bent on getting to the checkout window. It was probably fortunate that she also had substantial hearing loss. Daughter Emily took me aside and said, "I've been worried about Mom for a few months. She always sets an extra plate at the table on Saturday evening because..." she hesitated a bit, "she thinks Lawrence Welk is coming to dinner. She'd never put food on the plate before, but now she's giving him a helping of everything! What can I do—she's wasting a lot of food!" Never faced with this somewhat perplexing question before, I groped for an answer. "Well, Emily. I suppose you should just plan on Mr. Welk's portion being leftovers for you the next day? Perhaps you should tell your mother that Lawrence is eating dinner with another Champagne Lady tonight before the show."

WHAT'S THAT AGAIN?

Among the many families of patients at the Broad Street Clinic whose personal and medical challenges proved memorable, the Bates family was prominent. Billy Bates, Sr. was a hardy soul who had lived into his fifth decade as an employee of a local canning factory in spite of several handicaps. When I first saw Bill as a patient, he had nondescript complaints: shoulder pain, breathing problems, and loss of hearing. Within the first minutes of his history, I had a clear idea of contributing causes. His job required repetitive use of his arms and shoulders, he was exposed to perpetual noise in his work environment, and he'd been smoking two packs of cigarettes a day for over forty years.

However, it was his peculiar seated posture that puzzled me. He wore, as many of my older overweight male patients did, baggy overalls. But when seated, he always maintained a unique cross-legged position. Nothing in his immediate history clarified that peculiarity. However, on his physical exam, the lights came on. His shoulder showed the typical findings of chronic rotator cuff injury. He had "high mileage lungs", my euphemistic description of the early finding of chronic lung disease from a lifetime of smoking. And his ears, although they looked normal, demonstrated a typical pattern of high frequency neurologic damage from long term noise exposure. But the reason for his cross-leggedness was an anatomic one. Mr. Bates had the largest inguinal hernia I'd ever seen. After I discovered it, he recounted several failed attempts at having it repaired in the distant past. After the third or fourth time, he decided to simply live with a hernia roughly the size of a volley ball! Sitting with his legs together was a literal physical impossibility! After discussing some of the potential complications of this, but more importantly, dealing with his other more pressing complaints, I filed this mega-hernia among the several issues that needed to be monitored carefully in his future visits. Mr. Bates' response to our plan was a grudgingly accepting one. He wanted some pain pills to fix his shoulder and an inhaler to help his breathing. Like many long term smokers, he was stubbornly reluctant to modify what had become a vital but deadly aspect of daily life. He was perfectly content to watch the hernia.

Mr. Bates' wife Betty had been a patient of mine for years. A faithful and tolerant soul, she was careful about monitoring her diabetes and was compulsive about keeping careful lists of her blood sugar readings, bringing in a meticulous, penciled list of those readings every visit. But seeing her husband for the first time explained one factor that always had puzzled me. Why did she always talk so loud? Even our examination room conversations behind a closed door were easily audible to my medical assistants working outside in the hall. Thirty-five years of marriage to a man with Billy's diminished auditory acuity had made her constantly fortissimo speaking voice a requirement!

But the full explanation of Betty's speaking voice wasn't entirely clear until I saw their son, Billy Junior several years later. Junior had fallen through the cracks in the local educational system and had dropped out of school soon after his sixteenth birthday. In those days, schools were less accommodating to students with multiple handicaps. Junior's combination of limited intellectual resources and extreme nearsightedness was compounded by a profound hearing loss. Still living at home at nineteen, Billy Junior had been evaluated for his visual problem and wore corrective lenses that were of limited help. But his hearing, most likely a severe nerve-related loss in early childhood had not been corrected. It had been at least ten years since he had last received attention for this hearing problem, so with the approval and urging of both Billy Sr. and Betty, I arranged for an audiology exam. Both parents were understandably weary of the stentorian speaking tones that were required for family discussions. Even drawing out the plan for an audiology exam was daunting. I tried to explain that it was a special hearing test that would clarify what kind of help Junior might need to correct some of his hearing problem. However, it soon became clear that explanation had been inadequate.

The afternoon of Junior's audiology exam, I heard an overhead page from the telephone desk, "Dr. Johnston, a call on line three from the hospital". As I answered,

I heard an unfamiliar but desperate voice whispering, "Dr. Johnston? This is Dorothy in the patient advocate office. I need some help in dealing with the Bates family!" By that time, even over the phone, I could hear Mr. Bates' voice in the background. "The audiology lab sent them here because they were demanding that the son get a hearing aide today! I can't seem to get them to understand that won't happen now! They can't *hear* me!" Dorothy continued. As reassuringly as I could, I said, "Let me talk with Mr. Bates." Bill seemed to recognize my voice and after a few minutes, he understood that the exam Junior had today was to *prepare* for a correction in the future. Like many other Broad Street Clinic patients, Mr. Bates was intolerant of being put off and in this case, having frustrated expectations.

In the following years, Junior had several attempts at hearing correction with amplification, mostly of little or no help. Several years later, through the help of a college friend, now an otolaryngologist who had been instrumental in introducing the then dramatic possibility of cochlear implants to correct profound hearing loss, Junior became one of the first success stories for that new technology. Billy Sr., however was never a candidate for this benefit and on last report, was still occupying two chairs in the waiting room because of the breadth of leg room required by his gigantic hernia.

INTERLUDE II: POVERTY AND THE FAMILY

As virtually all these medical vignettes illustrate, inner city life and poverty—often interconnected by webs of cause and effect—have a profound effect on individuals. But inevitably, poverty has a significant effect on families as well. Much as social scientists struggle with complexities in explaining causes of inner city poverty for individuals, the causes and effects of poverty on families are multilayered and diverse.

During my forty years of practice, several issues have emerged as common contributors to the challenges of health care for families in poverty. Fragmentation and dysfunction of families in poverty often begins with the absence of fathers or even a father figure. Sadly, this is frequently the result of adolescent pregnancy when the father is unwilling or simply unable to provide financial or emotional support. Causes of unplanned or unwanted pregnancies in young girls are also multifactorial, but often the young mother herself has not known affection from a father and responds predictably to such attention by any male with sexual submission. What follows is dropping out of school, interruption in preparation for adulthood and employment, frequent dependence on maternal grandmother for both child care and guidance in healthcare. I still recall a patient of mine in her late thirties, walking into the examination area with her fourteen-year-old daughter who had just had her first baby. My patient was carrying her grand-child when she looked over at me and said, "Look what we did!" Adolescent pregnancy with its attendant consequences looms large on the list of significant influences of poverty on families and their healthcare.

As both the Allen and Whitaker families illustrated, (see Mom In A Jar and What About the Whitakers) a well-meaning but *dictatorial* father or mother can profoundly control the stability and vitality of families in poverty, directly affecting their health and access to health care. Mr. Allen's insecurity and sense of vulner-ability as manufacturing jobs gave way to more service-oriented jobs was translated into being hypercritical and controlling of his own children. Mrs. Whitaker's well-meaning micromanaging and control of her fam-ily's care and resources isolated them from friends and neighbors, alienating them from appropriate relation-ships and distancing them from the healthcare com-munity. As is often the case for families living in pov-erty, they lived for the moment and weren't able to order their resources to give health care an appropri-ate priority or to comply with advice to improve their health. Some families who struggle with even limited expenditures for medications to treat chronic diseases still find funds to purchase lottery tickets and ciga-rettes, another unfortunate lifestyle habit that adversely affects their health.

An even deeper problem that leaves a destructive scar on families is substance abuse. Alcohol and other illegal substances are often adopted by individuals with families in poverty as crutches to help cope with the stresses of those responsibilities. Drug and alcohol use clearly plays a role in family as well as personal dysfunction, contributing to job loss, financial drain, and adverse health consequences. It destroys hope. It destroys families. Drug and alcohol use destroys poten-tials in individuals. It can cause an impoverished com-munity to devour itself. [6]

Families who have a member with a chronic dis-ease or a child with behavioral or learning disabilities commonly become completely focused on care for that person, a consuming activity when poverty limits their options—in transportation, specialized care, or therapy. As Ava and Emily Barnes illustrated (see Lawrence Welk Comes To Dinner), sometimes a style of life is found, which allows living within means available with a chronic disease such as schizophrenia. However fami-lies who are limited by major sensory deficits—visual or hearing (as in the case of the Bates family - see What's That Again?)—are often left perpetually in need, lack-ing the skills or resources available as families in pov-erty to access or utilize the help available. An otherwise productive family leader such as David McMillan (see A Profound Arrhythmia) who becomes the victim of a disabling condition is frequently launched on a relentless downward spiral from which recovery is daunting.

And, it has been my observation that recurrent dysfunction over multiple generations of families can evolve into a lifestyle of poverty. In my Broad Street Clinic practice, I am now seeing the third generation of many families most of whom are still *stuck* in a culture of poverty. The families they've grown up in have never known anything but the ever-present threat of want. What fuels this *culture of poverty*? It is not just financial need. Educational needs are pervasive but not the only factor. Lack of family cohesion? Almost universal, but not limited to poverty. And health needs are not unique. The diseases I've seen in forty years of medical care in the inner city are basically the same maladies afflicting the communities surrounding the inner city. But poverty's effect on families touches all these areas. Families live with acute, urgent, short term focuses. Healthcare is lower on the list of priorities, particularly if it includes preventive care for potential diseases not yet symptomatic that could shorten life or diminish function. Max Moore (see A Rash With Risks) and his family were far less concerned about what a cholesterol over five hundred meant in regard to the risk of his having a heart attack. Max simply wanted his bothersome rash to disappear—and his family rewarded that desire with a Big Mac!

THE AMAZING WORLD
OF OBSTETRICS

As is true of all family physicians, I was trained in obstetrics during my residency. More than that, I had the good fortune to have a part-time job even as a medical student moonlighting as backup OB anesthetist in a large multispecialty hospital. In the late '60s and early '70s, it was still common practice to administer nitrous oxide and oxygen as a light anesthetic during delivery for normal pregnancies. Over the years, I participated in hundreds of deliveries from the *head end*, comforting women as they gave birth with a pain-relieving mask. The practice of OB is almost uniformly a gratifying one, but the lack of diversity kept me from choosing that as a specialty. I thoroughly enjoyed delivering babies and planned to do OB as I began my clinic practice.

However, reality soon prevailed. Being called urgently to the hospital five miles from my clinic in the middle of a busy afternoon to do a delivery when the waiting room was full of expectant patients was too disruptive. The only obstetrics care I did after the first year (with rare exceptions) was to diagnose pregnancy and provide referral for prenatal care. Even with that restricted perspective, OB provided some of my most memorable patient encounters.

Maggie Collins was a forty-eight-year-old woman who'd been one of my first clinic patients because of her severe diabetes and high blood pressure. She was obese, but still managed to work as a waitress at a nearby greasy spoon. She was faithful in taking her medications and in coming in for exams. She had lived for twenty-five years with her common law husband who was twenty years older than she, but she had never been able to get pregnant. On one of her diabetic visits, she mentioned that her periods had stopped. Since she was already forty-eight with her other medical conditions, menopause would be the most likely cause. I reassured her that it must be the case but decided to do a pregnancy test anyway. To my utter surprise, it was *positive*! I was so sure she could not be pregnant (because those early urine pregnancy tests were not one hundred percent accurate) that I did a blood pregnancy test. My concern deepened when that also was positive. I saw Maggie back a couple days later and she was ecstatic! To be pregnant for the first time at forty-eight was a miracle to her of Abrahamic proportions! I was most concerned because of the astronomically high risk factors of her advanced age and complicating medical conditions. She was undaunted. In fact, a few weeks later, she and her common law husband Tom were officially married! Her obstetrician, in spite of Maggie's pre-eclampsia and worsening blood pressure, was able to usher her through the first thirty-six weeks of pregnancy before doing a C-section. No child could have been more welcomed into a family than little Karen. Her development was delayed, but her mother and father, older than most grandparents would have been to her, loved her unconditionally, even though she had only a five-word vocabulary by the time she was four years old.

Most primary care physicians see occasional "immaculate conceptions", or unexpected pregnancies, in a woman who claims she hasn't had sex. My first few years of practice were sprinkled with such patients. Maria was one of the earliest and most dramatic of those for me. She was a very pleasant eighteen-year-old Hispanic high school senior, moderately overweight, who was brought in by her mother because her periods had stopped some indeterminate time before. It was clear that neither Maria nor her mother had communicated much about this but her mother was confident that Maria could not been active sexually—she didn't even have a boyfriend.

Just in looking at Maria, I suspected she was pregnant even before I examined her. When I palpated her abdomen, it was easy to feel what appeared to be a nearly full term pregnancy, and as I kept a hand on her belly, there were obvious, active fetal movements! Maria and I had a short conversation (in English), which her mother did not understand. As I calculated how long it had actually been since she'd had a period, it turned out that day was her *due date*! I asked her how she planned to let her mother know, and we decided to tell her together; I would talk to the mother in English, and Maria would translate. I started by saying that sometimes, pregnancies happen the first time a girl has sex and that it can be a result of the passion of the moment. Maria translated that first sentence, and then an animated conversation began in Spanish lasting several minutes to which *I* was not privy! There were many dramatic hand gestures, loud phrases that could only have been Spanish expletives and finally, tears from both Maria and her mother. I faded into the background as mother and daughter caught up on at least nine months of inadequate communication. Maria, in spite of a total absence of prenatal care, delivered a healthy baby boy three days later.

Agnes was another patient with an unusual contrasting obstetrical presentation. Her first visit was with her mother-in-law, a well-dressed woman in her mid-forties. Agnes had married this lady's youngest son the April before. They had wanted to start a family right away and, to the entire family's delight, Agnes's periods stopped in July. It was fall now and the mother-in-law had just bought her a beautiful maternity dress. Joy abounded. They came in to have a confirmatory test and to obtain prenatal care from our nurse-midwives. Agnes affirmed that her belly was getting bigger; she offhandedly mentioned that she'd also been having some diarrhea. I had her get a urine sample for a pregnancy test, but even before getting the result back, I examined her abdomen. In expected fashion, there was a five month or more size presumed uterine enlargement, palpable to near her belly button.

Congratulating them on this happy event, I proceeded to listen for fetal heart tones with a fetoscope. Nothing. There was no reassuring rapid heartbeat to be heard. I somewhat nervously moved the scope around various spots over her abdomen. Still, crickets. As I broke out in a slight sweat, the medical assistant handed me the pregnancy test through the door. Negative. Now I was really alarmed. I told Agnes that not hearing fetal heart tones wasn't unusual at this point (this was in the days of the old fetoscopes with ear pieces and a metal bell placed over the uterus while braced on the physician's head.) The negative pregnancy test was a bit concerning. She agreed to have a pelvic exam to more clearly define what was going on, and her mother-in-law stepped out of the room while we prepared Agnes for a gynecologic exam. As I began the exam, I realized to my chagrin what was happening. I could barely do a bimanual exam because there was a volley ball sized *stool impaction* in her rectum! Her uterus was small, pushed up against her bladder. It was a classic case of pseudocyesis—false pregnancy. Agnes's strong desire to get pregnant had precipitated the series of events including the cessation of periods and the stool backup.

As sympathetically as I knew how, I explained to Agnes that indeed she was *not* pregnant but *seriously constipated*. The diarrhea she mentioned was a clue to the stool problem she was having—stool leaking around the impaction. At first disbelieving and tearful, Agnes gradually expressed understanding of what had happened. However, when her mother-in-law reentered the room, she was incensed, first at me, then at

Agnes for perpetrating this embarrassing event. Not the least of her complaints was the expensive maternity dress she'd bought for her *constipated* daughter-in-law.

A final example, the drama of Mrs. Foster made all my other obstetrical adventures pale by comparison. My unplanned relationship with her began with an urgent phone call on a frigid January afternoon. At the time, our burgeoning prenatal program staffed by a part-time obstetrician and supported by several highly competent nurse practitioners had moved to a free-standing double-wide trailer at the back edge of our parking lot. Space demands made this arrangement a temporary necessity. The call came from the trailer, "Send Dr. Johnston here right away! We've got a pre-term labor going fast, and the obstetrician's not here!" I dropped what I was doing and raced out the door, shocked by the cold wind and single digit temperature. Hands under my arms, I heard muffled screams from the trailer even before I ran up the steps and burst through the door, now held open by a wide-eyed nurse. "She's going to deliver here!" she stammered. Inside the door on a rumpled gurney lay a still mostly dressed young woman in the final throes of a labor contraction that had been going on for over five minutes. There was blood all over the sheets as the woman continued screaming with a relentless contraction. The years since my last delivery seemed like decades as I pulled on a pair of surgical gloves and moved to the end of the gurney. *What do I do first? What about instruments?* Suddenly, all my questions were blotted out by the rapid delivery of a tiny baby boy, a gush of blood—and the placenta, still dangling from the umbilical cord! One powerful contraction proved it had to be a placental abruption, dangerous for the mother, often lethal for the baby. As I observed the baby in my hands, he was limp, bluish, not breathing. I could detect a faint pulse—Apgar 1? [7]

To my undying relief, the young pediatrician who had just joined our practice had followed not far behind me into the trailer and calmly took over the care of the baby. She inserted a tiny endotracheal tube and administered oxygen that prompted a gasp for air; the baby's color improved immediately and he started flailing all four extremities! With the delivery of baby and placenta, the bleeding had stopped, and when the ambulance arrived, baby and mother were transported to the hospital for evaluation and aftercare. As I walked back to the clinic building, the heat of the moment made the chill outdoor temperature feel welcome.

In a surprising epilogue, it was five years later that I was again seeing patients on a Monday evening. My first patient was an attractive young woman whose new chart reflected that I'd never seen her before. The appointment was for a routine checkup that occupied only fifteen minutes or so. When I finished the exam, the woman asked a question with a sly smile on her face, "Dr. Johnston, do you still do OB?" I told her it had been over twenty years since I'd practiced obstetrics during that first year of clinic practice. She smiled further and said, "Oh no, you did some OB just five years ago!" At first, I couldn't understand what she meant, but then it slowly dawned on me and a faint recollection returned—of that one cold winter day I was running across the parking lot! I had never seen her after that gut-wrenching episode, but indeed, it was Mrs. Foster who had delivered her son so quickly in our OB trailer! "He just finished kindergarten and has been doing great!" No news could have been more welcome than this after her son's harrowing birth. But amazing events like this are among the compelling reasons making obstetrics such a rewarding practice!

MONDAY EVENING MADNESS

Health Education was a popular program in our clinic in the late '70s. There was optimism that by simply *educating* our patients with hypertension, diabetes, obesity, and smoking, they would have more ownership in their disease management and the complications of these common problems would diminish. Our clinic had a popular and energetic young lady who developed an imaginative program for Health Education, and it rapidly became one of our most effective outreaches. There were diabetic education programs on Wednesday mornings (when the vending machines for soft drinks and candy bars typically ran out), smoking cessation classes on Fridays and, a well-attended exercise hour on Monday evenings, which was personally led by our Health Educator, Susan.

Vickie was one of the most enthusiastic fans of the Monday evening exercise class. She also had bipolar disorder and when she was in a manic phase, would be very energetic and an irrepressible participant in the exercises, dancing frenetically to the music Susan piped in. But Vickie spent most of her time in a depressed mood, sometimes profoundly melancholic and was difficult to even engage in conversation. She responded moderately well to antidepressants and never had shown any suicidal tendencies.

One Monday evening I was preparing to begin clinic hours, expecting to see the usual and predictable collection of mostly blue collar working men who couldn't keep appointments during daytime hours. The exercise class had begun in the large room on the second floor of our clinic building, the former sanctuary of the original church building where our clinic was housed. As I was reading a chart preparing to enter an examination room, a breathless Susan rushed into the hall, stuttering. "Co-come quick! Vickie just shot herself!" I raced after Susan, expecting the worst and when I arrived, quickly thought those fears were realized. Vickie sat slumped against a wall at the edge of the exercise floor, clusters of terrified women in leotards huddled around her with hands to their mouths. When I kneeled down next to her, I saw to my horror that Vickie was bleeding profusely from a wound in her right temple. Although her eyes were closed at first, they suddenly fluttered open and she said, "I'm sorry. I just couldn't help myself. Everything's gone wrong..." I was astounded to see her open her eyes, much less hear her speak after what appeared to be a lethal wound, but I still took the precaution of gently taking the small-caliber hand gun from her right hand. The nurses behind me had brought the crash cart up the elevator, and I used some gauze to clean off the wound. Then, to my surprise, I saw what had to be an exit wound on *top* of her scalp, only a few inches from the entrance wound above her ear. As I heard the sirens from the approaching ambulance, it dawned on me that Vickie had aimed too high. The bullet had apparently burrowed under her scalp at a shallow angle and come out the top of her head without ever penetrating the skull! The arriving medics quickly took over and transported Vickie to the emergency room.

Vickie spent many weeks in the psychiatric unit after that incident, receiving multiple trials of medication, and engaging in group and individual therapy. Her course was a rocky one and although she had no other complicating medical problems, she never seemed to regain her previous level of function. She had no supportive family, and I saw her only sporadically after that event. She would come in once or twice a year for common colds, sore throats and, ironically, headaches. She continued to be profoundly depressed in spite of stronger and stronger medications, many of which caused side effects of emotional withdrawal and the facial flatness characteristic of these drugs. Sadly, I also noticed increasing numbers of scars on her arms where Vickie had tried repetitively to cut herself as a manifestation of her profound unhappiness. She became somewhat of a "fixture" in the neighborhood, often seen walking aimlessly up and down nearby streets and alleys, an unfortunate reflection of the increasing pressure to avoid chronic inpatient placement of psychiatric patients. Sometimes, I would see her sitting on the railing of an Interstate overpass near the Broad Street Clinic. If she was sitting with her feet on the side facing the street as I drove over the bridge, I'd roll down the window, greet her, and invite her to come to the clinic for a checkup. If she was sitting with her legs on the other side, *over* the traffic passing underneath, I'd call 911.

Mrs. Farris was another patient who memorably came only on Monday nights, because that's when her physician son could bring her. Her son was a friend of mine and had failed multiple attempts in finding a doctor his mother would accept. The last family doctor she'd seen six or eight times before coming to me had gone to the extent of giving back all the money she'd paid because "he hadn't done me any good!" I think he simply wanted to assure that she would never come back. After a visit or two, it became clear that Mrs. Farris had a major thought disorder, significant psychotic thinking, but she seemed to have succeeded in living alone for the decades after she'd been divorced. She was convinced she had a dreadful parasitic or viral infection and would often bring in nondescript barely visible debris that she'd extracted from her skin or bodily orifices to demonstrate her suspected cause of the disease. It also had caused her, she thought, to lose her teeth, and she'd periodically present me with a tooth or two, which she would rattle around in a small bottle as she loudly demanded that I diagnose and treat this terrible malady. A visit to the dental school confirmed that her tooth loss was simply from neglected pyorrhea. The few tests that I was able to do with her consent were uniformly negative. She absolutely refused to take any anti-psychotic medication. Her time demands were significant, and I finally negotiated with her a rigid, every three weeks, twenty-minute appointment schedule, which she kept meticulously. The mere thought of her coming in on those select Monday evenings was enough to elicit a Pavlovian tachycardia for me an hour before her arrival. My staff would hover worriedly outside the door of the exam room, ready to whisk me away as soon as the twenty minutes were up.

Strangely, Mrs. Farris's most significant therapeutic breakthrough came after a family tragedy. Her daughter, who long-sufferingly brought Mrs. Farris to appointments when her physician son was busy, had a new baby who unfortunately, had profound cerebral palsy. Mrs. Farris suddenly lost most of her preoccupation with her own real and imagined maladies, and poured herself into helping care for this new, handicapped child. The times between her appointments got longer and longer, initially to my puzzled delight, but later on to my amazement, when I saw the effect this new responsibility was having on her. She was drawn out of her old paranoia and anger in caring for this newborn granddaughter. Although both her son and daughter told me later that the sessions she'd had with me, ranting and angry, every three weeks for several years, had been more helpful than any medication she'd ever taken, I was still awed by how effective the therapy of helping a dependent child was on Mrs. Farris. Difficult patients like Mrs. Farris and Vickie are common in any medical practice. Most physicians work hard to minimize contact with such patients. In some respects, an inner city clinic practice is the "court of last resort" for many of these patients and referring, terminating, or transferring their care to another provider is difficult or impossible. Often, however, the best treatment is not in a pill bottle.

THE PLAGUE
OF CIGARETTES

The statistics are grim. Although the incidence of smoking cigarettes has declined nationwide to slightly over twenty percent since 1964, in the population of the Broad Street Clinic and many others like it across the country, that percentage has continued to hover stubbornly at over fifty percent. Nowhere have the tobacco companies been more successful at marketing their products than in the inner cities where the enticing images of success, romance, happiness, and athletic or outdoor prowess lure the casual observer into accepting the lie: cigarettes make life better. The hard truth is what I observe every day: smokers in my clinic population have at least a one in four chance of dying of a smoking-related disease and pay an incalculable cost not only in money but future health.

I probably spend more time discussing smoking issues with my patients than any other problem, justly earning the title one new patient gave me when I introduced myself. "Oh, I've heard about you, Dr. Johnston.

You're the 'Doctor That Hates Smoking!'" My reputation is justly deserved as one who would sometimes call the police to report a merchant. This would happen if I was waiting to pay for gas in a convenience store and saw a seven-year-old child, commonly one of my patients, in front of me in line being permitted to buy "for my Daddy" two packs of Marlboros! The incredible grip a smoking habit has on patients has been reinforced more times than I can count.

The history of a diabetic, pack-a-day smoker coming in to complain they couldn't afford their insulin anymore with blood sugars over four hundred is a more than yearly event. How many strokes have been caused by stopping blood pressure medicines in favor of maintaining their smoking habit? Yes, it's true that one memorable smoker (Rella–see Musical Interludes) showed incomprehensible ingenuity in finding a way to smoke in the locked psychiatric ward where she was hospitalized. In spite of weighing over two hundred ninety pounds and being slowed by arthritis, she managed to stand on her bedside table and puff a cigarette directly into her ceiling vent so "the nurses wouldn't smell the smoke!" She was also one who, some years later when her chronic lung disease had progressed to the point of requiring supplementary nasal oxygen, I found with dark unmistakable nicotine stains on her nasal oxygen cannula. I warned her (*I even showed her pictures!*) of instances of unintentional self-conflagration when an oxygen user forgot to turn off their flow before lighting up. The habit persisted. At her peak,

Rella claimed to be smoking seven packs a day which suggested that she was literally smoking while asleep.

However, the most memorable smoking saga began with a medical incident only obliquely related to cigarettes. Howard Drake was a middle school janitor who hadn't needed a doctor for over thirty years. His problems began during that health care black hole between Christmas and New Year's Day. He developed a persistent productive cough accompanied by fever, and after ten days, finally went to a local emergency room. After an appropriate exam including a chest X-ray, he was told he had pneumonia and was prescribed an antibiotic. Since he'd never been to Broad Street Clinic, it was his first to visit for a follow-up that January. Although he no longer had a fever, he was still coughing, and since we had to start from the beginning with him as a new patient, I took a more complete history.

It turned out that Mr. Drake, who was fifty-nine by then, had been smoking, since he was *three*! By the report he gave, his parents had been told (this must have been in the late '20s) by their well-meaning general practitioner that little Howard would have fewer spells of croup if they gave him three cigarettes to smoke every day. Accordingly, he was dutifully introduced, at a doctor's recommendation, to the smoking habit as a preschooler!

His current history that now included an episode or two of coughing up blood-tinged mucous prompted me to do both a TB skin test and another comparison chest X-ray. Frighteningly, his TB test was positive. Even more ominously, his chest X-ray showed some resolution of the pneumonia, but lurking in the background were two cavities in the upper part of that same lung. A finding sometimes associated with TB, this spotlighted a potential public health nightmare. I imagined four hundred middle school students, and twice that many parents who would soon be facing the reality of needing skin tests and screening after the risk of being innocently exposed to Howard's inadvertent infectious janitorial services.

Many tests followed, primarily, a collection of Mr. Drake's sputum to look for the unmistakable microscopic evidence of acid fast bacilli [8]. Although the initial tests were negative, I continued Howard's evaluation by referring him to a lung expert who could do a definitive test by bronchoscopy (looking through an instrument into his breathing tubes). Test followed test, and to my relief, and the relief of the entire school system, Mr. Drake did *not* have active TB. However, the ultimate diagnosis was even worse. His pneumonia was a result of germs being trapped upstream from a cancerous lung mass, which had blocked off the natural drainage system. Although surgery was entertained, the cancer had already spread to the lymph nodes between his lungs. Mr. Drake's outlook was dim. Within six months of my first seeing him, but fifty-seven years after he'd started smoking, Mr. Drake died at the age of sixty.

I wish I had some positive anecdotes to balance these dark ones. I only have a very few. There have been a few success stories—among the ten to fifteen percent of patients who tried to quit smoking and succeeded. My simplistic "Three Steps to Quitting" have born some fruit. First, set the *day* to quit smoking. Second, choose a replacement *crutch* to substitute for cigarettes in your everyday life, preferably something noncaloric and portable. Third, tell someone else you're going to *quit* and ask them to be your ally. A surprising number of grandchildren have been the ally that finally helped a Grandma stop! Occasional innovations arose. Another patient, Claude Emery told me he treated both his chronic lung disease *and* his desire to start smoking again by playing a tune on the open holes of his adjustable metal cane. Mrs. Bentley shared that she prepared pieces of plastic straws by stuffing them with cotton then breathing through them when she wanted to smoke. I encourage any creative way to give up this plague of a deadly habit.

COMMON OR UNCOMMON?

There is a strong temptation for physicians to make rapid diagnoses as they recognize familiar symptoms or physical findings of common disease entities. Many aphorisms support this: "When you hear hoof beats, look for horses, not zebras," or "Look for uncommon manifestations of common problems rather than common findings of uncommon problems." Nowhere is that rapid diagnostic recognition more common than in the field of dermatology.

The swath of a painful, always one-sided blistery rash that accompanies shingles, the common late manifestation of herpes zoster infection is unmistakable. Or, the sparse scatter of pearly white bumps that accompany the common childhood nuisance of *molluscum contagiosum* is another example of an instantly recognizable common disease.

Early in my years at the Broad Street Clinic diseases that were once common have now have fortunately become very rare or unheard of. In the sixties and seventies, a child with a fever of 104 degrees, a brassy cough, and a widespread red macular rash would be diagnosed with common measles. The diagnosis would be obvious within seconds of walking through the examination room door. Support for this entity could come from looking in the throat to see evidence of Koplik spots—a distinctive patchy whitish rash inside the cheeks. The only reason to actually use a stethoscope would be to assure that there was no associated pneumonia. Increasingly universal immunization has made this presentation extremely uncommon in the twenty-first century.

A less common but almost always quickly recognizable disease manifest by distinctive skin findings was illustrated by Marvin Coggins, the fiancée of a long time female patient of mine, Pearl Davis. It was in the days when to get a marriage license, residents of our state were required to have a serologic blood test for syphilis. Marvin and my patient were actually in the laboratory having their blood samples drawn when Pearl summoned me into the room as I walked by with a student. "Dr. Johnston, could you look at this rash Marvin has? It's been there for over a month and bothers him because it makes his hands sore." As we peered over at Marvin's rash, my dermatology warning bells were ringing, but I thought I'd test my student's expertise. "Doctor", (a complementary title, since he was technically still a senior medical student), "what do you think of this? Notice the red spots all over his arms are also on the palms of his hands."

Immediately, my student who had shown a proclivity for intimate evaluation of skin problems through the month by the touch-and-feel method began to palpate this man's palms. "Whoa! Let's discuss the differential before you go any further!" I said. "Well," he said, "I know hand dermatitis can look like this. And doesn't Rocky Mountain spotted fever show up with a rash on the palms and soles?" "Yes, but you're forgetting the most important one..." A blank look came on his face, followed by the wincing response of recognition. In a small voice, he said, "Uh, oh yes! Secondary syphilis. And it's contagious, isn't it?"

After my affirmation, he disappeared immediately to wash his hands! The results of Marvin's blood test confirmed with a strongly positive test for syphilis that he was entering marriage with a simultaneous need for penicillin shots! Marvin's demonstration of common findings of an uncommon condition was memorable.

However, Weston Adams deserves the most recognition as the one patient who repeatedly illustrated the common/uncommon conundrum. When I first met him, he was a shy fourteen-year-old who presented to our clinic for the first time with complaints of nervousness, shaking, and weight loss. As I walked into the room, I could tell he appeared apprehensive. Although I tried to put him at ease with the usual banter, he still appeared fearful, and I could detect a fine tremor. *Could he be hyperthyroid?* I'd never seen it in someone this young. But as I examined him, every finding began to fall in place with that diagnosis. He was rapier-thin at 108 lbs, 69 inches tall. His resting pulse was an astounding 140 beats per minute with a blood pressure of 170/108! In addition to the fine resting tremor, he had hyperactive muscle stretch reflexes, fine hair, and skin texture and, I thought, even a slight thyroid enlargement. With no other convincing explanations for these findings, I confidently ordered a thyroid blood panel, fully expecting the results to confirm my diagnosis of what I thought was an obvious condition.

Imagine my surprise when all his thyroid tests came back absolutely normal! I was still not convinced. When I saw him a second time two weeks later, findings were virtually the same. This time, I dug a little further into his social history. Although he seemed careful in answering, I didn't think he was being deceptive when he revealed no overt stress problems at home or at school. But with a blood pressure of 160/100 and his pulse still hovering above a hundred twenty, I felt compelled to begin treatment. I chose a beta blocker, propranolol, because of its ability to slow heart rate and lower blood pressure as well as to suppress tremor.

Weston came back two months later, taking propranolol with normal blood pressure and fewer tremors. But his resting pulse was still over a hundred. Dubious about his thyroid, I ordered a second round of blood tests. All were normal—again. Then, he dropped off the radar screen for over a year.

When I saw the request for a refill on his propranolol after eighteen months, I insisted that he come in for another exam. Later that week when I walked into his examination room, Weston was sitting on the edge of the exam table in a peculiar posture. Although he was sitting, his torso was tilted back as he supported his upper body on his arms. I'd already seen that he'd gained over thirty pounds since his last visit, but he retained that same thinness in his extremities. As I greeted him, although he shook my hand, he didn't sit forward; he maintained the strange backward tilted posture. The vital signs had a familiar look. Pulse: 120. Blood pressure: 140/98. But as I examined him and came to checking his abdomen, I was astounded. His entire abdomen was a firm *mass*. I'd never felt anything like it! The reason he couldn't sit up was that his belly was completely full of...something. The list of diagnostic possibilities was frighteningly short—and they were all *bad* possibilities—mostly associated with cancer. Then I did a rectal exam. Weston was exquisitely uncomfortable, but it showed he had an impaction of world-class proportions. I could hardly believe the mass filling his entire abdomen could represent such a gigantic stool impaction and made preparations for a referral to a pediatric gastroenterologist. Several months later, I got a detailed letter from my friend, Dr. Foley who described a similar incredulous response to Weston's workup. Dr. Foley is a world-renowned authority in his specialty. He had evaluated Weston literally from top to bottom. He was so sure that this must represent an unusual form of Hirschprung Disease (a rare, usually hereditary disorder of the enervation of the colon, associated with massive stool backups and inability to move the bowels) that he actually did a biopsy of the colon wall looking for evidence of that abnormality. Although it took the better part of two weeks in the hospital, Weston finally came through with an entirely negative workup. The best they could offer was that he represented a unique case of encopresis—voluntary stool withholding. His GI system tested *normal* in every respect. Neither one of us had ever seen this relatively common condition of such severity in an older teenager. Or was there something truly uncommon going on that neither of us had discovered?

Then, Weston disappeared completely for over two years. Requests for refills of his propranolol ceased. I worried that something dreadful had happened. Finally he re-emerged, showing up for a visit regarding, of all things, back pain. Strangely, he'd gained fifty pounds, his resting pulse was under eighty and his blood pressure was normal. The exam of his back was normal, and his abdomen was also normal. As I took his history further, he mentioned that he'd moved away from home and had his own job. When I asked if he was still in touch with his mother and father, Weston paused and I noted a faraway look in his eye. He then went on to explain the rest of the story, painfully recalling the reasons why he stopped the visits. "Ever since I was ten years old, after my mother remarried, my step dad was sexually molesting me—at least every week," he said in a flat voice. As he recounted those years of unimaginable pain, trying to *protect* his mother, it became obvious what was behind his prior findings. Fears of being discovered kept his heart racing—emotional revulsion and physical pain at his sexual molestation led to the stool withholding. We had simply never asked the right questions to permit his history to be revealed!

OUTSIDE THE DOOR STORIES

One of the observations I shared with students had an only indirect relationship to medicine. After practicing at the Broad Street Clinic for over twenty years, I found out that I had to go at least a mile away from my clinic for lunch; otherwise, all the waitresses would be my patients and there'd be unofficial checkups! Although this wasn't literally true, there were more times than I could count when, while being served in one of the many small Ma and Pa restaurants nearby, I'd be faced with the awkward reality of having to provide an informal *consult* over a bowl of chili for a patient or patient's relative. ("Aunt Vi, show the doctor that lump on your leg!") Variations of those outside-the-clinic-doors contacts could be as diverse as a family of tittering children pointing at me in the nearby grocery while whispering loudly to their mother, "*Look* mom, there's Doctor Johnston!" Then there was a young man who was actually willing to *show* me the genital findings he thought represented a venereal disease while we were standing beside my car in the parking lot! The most recent recognition experience occurred in the unlikely context of accompanying our grandchildren to a local museum. One of the docents, unrecognizable to me at first, was a former clinic employee of twenty years before. Her hesitant question when she recognized me was, "Didn't you...used to be a doctor?" It was a bit unnerving to be faced even *before* retirement with the question, "Am I only what I do?"

Other outdoor vignettes were memorable both for medical *and* non-medical reasons. On a hot summer afternoon as I was leaving the clinic to drive home, a woman I'd not seen before was coming toward the door, holding her throat and obviously in distress. Her voice was barely audible as she said, "I need help. This is a clinic, isn't it?" Even before I could say yes, she went on. "I just got stung by a yellow jacket, and I'm allergic. I...can h-hardly breathe..." and her voice trailed off, muffled by what I knew must have been the relentless advance of anaphylaxis—a deadly allergic cascade. As she stumbled along behind me, my mind raced ahead. The rest of the staff was gone and I was alone. I knew there was some adrenalin in the crash cart, but should I call 911 immediately? We got to the nurses' station together, and she seemed a bit more comfortable inside where it was air conditioned. It took only ten seconds to get the syringe out and give her 1 cc of adrenalin, the quickest way to turn off an anaphylactic reaction. As soon as I finished the injection, I dialed 911. Within only a minute, her symptoms began to abate. By the time the emergency medics arrived with the ambulance, she was virtually back to normal. It was one of the few times when my reason for getting home late, a fortunately rare occurrence, was a legitimate life saving one!

Some encounters in an outdoor environment were different, hard to categorize any other way. There was the peculiar time when we had a caller who wanted to bring Fred Moser for an exam because his knee hurt. A patriarch of the family, he was a massive man of nearly four hundred pounds. However, they warned us that he couldn't walk and they were bringing him in a truck. Fred arrived, agonizing on a mattress in the back of a rusting pickup truck where I examined him. Although it was not the usual clean environment of a medical examination room, it wasn't hard to make the diagnosis. His knee was red, hot, and swollen; he said it was excruciatingly painful to move. Usually a single red joint like this *could* be gout; but with a fever of 102 degrees, I was virtually sure that it was septic arthritis—an emergency situation that demands immediate hospitalization. Fred's ambulance was the family pickup.

Other interactions in the community involved mixed medical and social relationships. Among my many patients are a handful of women who describe their occupation as "dancer". Occasionally, this includes a moonlighting job predisposing to high risks of sexually transmitted disease. Predictably, in a global sense, these women go out of their way to fit the alluring mold of their profession. Sometimes, but not often, their dress during clinic visits would reflect this. Amy was one of these women whom I had seen for several different problems, none of them serious or contagious. But Amy had a uniquely effusive, friendly personality. She was never one to mask her affection, specifically in a greeting. Parallel to understanding this particular encounter with Amy, it would be important to know that I've made it a habit to meet with a handful of close friends, physicians, and others once a month or so over breakfast or lunch as part of my personal growth and accountability. One nonmedical friend met me in this fashion at a casual eatery right across the street from the county court offices. It was a noisy gathering spot where hundreds of lunch-goers met to eat and chat. Many of the patrons were connected with the court system, so it wasn't unusual to see attorneys, jury members, and even judges, eating there. Some were, needless to say, those who came involuntarily because of legal constraints. This lunch date with my male friend was memorably interrupted by Amy, who was dressed in her voluptuous best. When she saw me, she swerved to stop at our table and leaned over dangerously. "Why, Doctor Johnston, imagine seeing you here! Could you maybe eat with *me* sometime?" she gushed. I haltingly introduced Amy to my friend, David, whose expression suggested significant incredulity! I later found out from Amy that she'd just been in court to deal with a charge of "solicitation."

My favorite community vignette arose in a setting not at all connected with my official medical relationships. For many years, I went to a barber whose shop adjoined a small Christian bookstore he owned and ran. It was a warm, welcoming place, often a gathering spot for the good ol' boys of the neighborhood, friends of the barber and more particularly, fellow church members of a nearby inner city church. It was several miles from my clinic, so I was just a young man of totally unknown background who had simply chosen the shop for haircuts. During the first year I patronized this establishment, I had the somewhat unsettling experience of having the barber tell me, "I'll be gone next month for several weeks, but my Dad will be here to take my place." I thought it was a bit unusual since he was at least sixty-five at the time, making his father likely eighty-five or older! Sure enough, I was greeted by a twenty-year-older version of my barber when I arrived the next month. He assured me that he'd also spent his working life as a barber, so much of my apprehension was quelled—until I saw his hands. He had a tremor of astounding proportions! I had many patients with Parkinsonism, but most had much less of a tremor than this man. I almost had a vision of clippers bogged down on my head while his shaking hand cropped hair off in ragged chunks. Thankfully, he did a commendable work! I was amazed by how well he could control his tremor.

To appreciate the final episode, it's vital to know that at the time, I was driving an old, rusted, compact station wagon. I think it even had the propensity to emit smoke from the exhaust pipe occasionally. It had reached the point that the only reason I locked it was to keep someone from putting something I didn't want *in* it. A year before, I had discovered a paper bag of old clothes in the back seat and never did discover where they'd come from or who put them there! On the day of that memorable haircut, I drove in hurriedly and found a group of men, all the barber's church friends, engaged in an animated discussion. As I sat down in the barber chair, it quickly became clear they were discussing their church's recent fund drive for a building. As the conversation progressed, the following interchange took place. "Yep, I think we'll make it to our goal by the end of next month." Another one said, "We'd already be there if Doctor Jones gave as much as he could! Seems t' me that them docs never give much. As much as they *could* at least, considerin' how much they *make!*" Then the third man spoke up, "We'd better be careful, who knows! This guy in the chair might be a doctor." (laughter) But my barber spoke up, "Oh no! He's not a doctor. Did you see the kind of car he drove in?" (more laughter) Then the barber added, "What *do* you do?" After a period of reflective silence, I finally spoke up. "Well, I actually *am* a physician at the Broad Street Clinic north of here..." It was as if I'd been struck deaf. There was absolute silence as the group of gathered men quietly replayed their memory tapes of the last minutes of conversation. "Don't feel bad. I agree that we docs are expected to—and should—give a lot," I broke in. "But, you see. I give enough to *my* church that I can't afford a new car..."

INTERLUDE III: POVERTY AND THE COMMUNITY

Reflect with me for one last time as I offer a glimpse of poverty from a different perspective— its effect on community and healthcare. This time, demographics are involved. The people making up the community around the Broad Street Clinic are a mix of Appalachian and African-Americans, with an increasing number of Hispanics. An unfortunate statistic is that as pure *racial* segregation has diminished (since 1970), segregation of the *poor* has increased. Suburbanization of jobs and the middle class has left inner city residents isolated from the economic and cultural mainstream. When I began my practice, many former inner city medical practitioners were following this suburbanization pattern leaving the poor community even more bereft of primary health care.

Scrutiny of several aspects of the impact of poverty on community healthcare could be instructive. When I started my practice in the mid-seventies, the infant death rate (deaths per thousand live births) was over twenty-five—worse than some Iron Curtain countries at the time! A good friend of mine looked carefully at the cost of caring for these high-risk infants and compared that to the cost of early prenatal care. It soon became clear that investing in community-based and personalized prenatal care could have a profound effect on improving infant survival. When the local county health system was provided with these statistics, a comprehensive and innovative program of prenatal care cut the infant death rate in half within five years and saved hundreds of thousands of dollars in care for premature infants! At the heart of this system with astoundingly positive results were the nurses who connected with each pregnant patient and often visited them in their homes and community. The detrimental effect poverty had had previously in preventing early and effective prenatal care was overcome by a community based program.

Another arena where poverty, community, and health care intersect is the pernicious habit of cigarette smoking. As elaborated in The Plague of Cigarettes, smoking is the most important preventable cause of death and disease in the inner city community. But no community can prevent situations such as this. One afternoon, I saw a child with a severe asthma flare up, whose mother smoked but claimed she never smoked *indoors*. No more than an hour after seeing them, I was wolfing down a quick sandwich at a nearby fast food restaurant when I saw her approaching the drive-up window in a pickup truck—smoking—with her child in the front seat (apparently not *indoors*)! Disturbing as this vignette may be, the number of intractable smokers who have quit has slowly been increasing. This fact is due in no small way to communities that permit smoking in fewer public places, as well as the increasing incentives to promote smoking cessation.

Education is a community resource that has a profound influence on poverty. Too often, it is not valued by families living in poverty; and the available schools essential to providing quality education are degraded by outdated facilities, lack of funding, and teachers who are discouraged and devalued. As the labor market increasingly favors the educated over the blue-collar workers, the number of workers achieving a high school education in poverty-stricken communities has diminished. In the general population, only about twenty-five percent of folks over twenty-five years of age have a less than twelve-year education. Among those living in inner city, almost sixty percent of people over twenty-five have completed fewer than twelve years of school. Functional illiteracy is rampant in poor districts. Increasing numbers of entry-level jobs are taken by new immigrants, trapping the poor inner city residents in cycles of unemployment and despair.

The issue of poverty and community involvement in mental health care also deserves consideration. The Broad Street Clinic is part of a system that has a Homeless Initiative Program. A large number of our homeless patients have significant chronic mental illnesses, and these illnesses contribute to homelessness and complicate health care. As medications for treating chronic mental illness have improved, the number of facilities to house these patients for long-term care has dwindled to virtually nothing. Many of these patients are now expected to be managed through Mental Health Clinics and cared for by family or in group homes. This also tends to be a self-perpetuating problem with no easy answers. The stories told in Lawrence Welk Comes to Dinner and Monday Madness illustrate this complex poverty/community interaction.

Past efforts with Medicaid/Medicare to meet some of the health care needs of those in poverty at a community level met mixed success. The disparity of funding for health care in inner city communities is one factor that has kept many providers from venturing into these communities as a career. Public policies intending to alleviate social problems have too often had unanticipated negative consequences, thus worsening the problem over the long term. We can only hope that the Healthcare Reform/Affordable Healthcare Act will offer a new breath of life for the healthcare of poverty communities.

MEMORABLE MALAPROPISMS

Unending months of the stress of finding an affordable treatment for relentless chronic diseases, juggling the nuances of an expensive diagnostic workup, and searching for the *right* consultant to help with a complex case can make the life of an inner city physician emotionally exhausting. When it seems like there's no relief in sight, the unexpected humor of a medical malapropism can be delightfully therapeutic for everyone! Sometimes, the unintentional blunder in word or action is on the part of the physician. For instance at the end of a tiring day, while doing a hernia exam on a teenage boy, using the routine phrase, "Say ahh" (more appropriate for looking in a throat) instead of "Now, cough." Or the titters of laughter I heard from a Hispanic sixteen-year-old after a visit with her mother for an exam for contraception, giving them a patient education pamphlet, written in Spanish, expecting it had to do with birth control, only to find out I'd given them instructions on treating head lice!

All medical care givers get used to the *usual suspects* in medical term mispronunciations: confusing the 'ynx words *larnix* and *pharnix* and the male organ, the *prostrate*. It is the totally unexpected verbal faux pas that generate the lip-biting humor, sometimes shared with the patients, other times retained for colleague reprise. I was writing a note near the front desk one day when a middle-aged man came there and confidently asked the receptionist to see the *mirage nurse*. Our triage nurses wouldn't have appreciated being relegated to an imaginary status!

Other verbal misfires sometimes occurred in the more private arena of the examination room. When I saw the chief complaint of a twenty-six-year-old man listed as, "Swelling of the Biloxies," I was puzzled. All became clearer when I found that he had epididmytis (infection and swelling of the area around the testicles) and I understood that *biloxies* must have been a euphemism that he grew up with in his family or culture. It never occurred to me to ask if it had anything to do with an unfortunate sexual tryst in the like-named gulf coast Mississippi town.

Similarly, I was pushed to stifle a guffaw when a new patient, a fifty-four-year-old man, was struggling to remember part of his family history. He said his mother had been diagnosed recently with a visual condition that he thought might be important. After a protracted period of thinking, his face lit up. "Oh yes, it was 'immaculate deception,'" he exclaimed, proud of thinking of such a technical word! After a few puzzled seconds of mental head scratching, the light dawned on me. "Ohhh! You mean *macular degeneration*?" Pleased, he said, "Oh yes, that's it! I knew it had an *m* and a *d* in it!"

Scattered over the years were many less memorable phrases, like the lady who, during the flu season, was sure she had "gutter flu," which in her estimation was far worse than swine flu or Spanish flu. I assured her that they were *all* caused by viruses and that she probably wouldn't need penicillin after all.

But Angel Trueblood was the creator of what is still the most thought provoking mystery name in recent memory. Angel was one of my many smoking patients with such severe chronic lung disease that I am quick to start an antibiotic if they have an abrupt increase in productive cough with fever. She had both complaints for nearly a week when I saw her. "Dr. Johnston, I think I need a chest X-ray this time. But while you're at it, could you also have them get an X-ray of my 'Zacharias?'" she said. I'd already checked off *PA Chest X-ray* on the requisition, but I knew I wouldn't find "Zacharias" among the other body parts. At first, I thought she could have a close male friend and fellow smoker named Zacharias who might be similarly deserving of a chest X-ray; but I was familiar with the name as one of the prophets in the Old Testament and knew it was a highly unlikely modern day name. "Angel, I'm not sure what or who your 'Zacharias' is. Could you help me?" I asked after much contemplation. "Oh yes," she answered and pointed down at the area behind her left hip on the lower back. "This is my 'Zacharias' and it's been hurting like mad, especially when I roll over in bed at night!" *Aha, she means her sacroiliac! That makes sense.* "Do you mean your *sacroiliac*, Angel? That's right there where you're pointing." "Oh yeh! *Sacroiliac, Zacharias*—whatever it is! It hurts me, and I'd like you to make it better!" As I recall, both X-rays were negative, but I still had a dreadful time finding a legitimate ICD-9 diagnostic code number for "sore Zacharias!"

UNEXPECTED RESULTS

Diversity was one of the attributes of family medicine that attracted me to the specialty forty years ago—the unending array of backgrounds, personalities, and particularly diagnoses that are on the everyday menu of practice at the Broad Street Clinic. The fascinating palette of findings in each patient (if arranged sensibly), contributes to a final diagnosis that brings satisfaction and sometimes spontaneous humor, which make the practice of medicine not just a science but also an art..

Unexpected findings are, by their very nature, the *eureka moments* that memorably contribute to a comprehensible whole. Almost every day, those surprising nuggets emerge in inner city practice. Often, a glaringly abnormal laboratory test is where it starts.

One of our nurse practitioners came to me one day to consult on a patient she was seeing. Her concern was an unusual rash. Dorothy, the patient was a sixteen-year-old girl who had just moved back to her home town from Florida because she'd been doing poorly in school and her mom thought the Midwest might be friendlier to her academic achievement. Her general medical history was unremarkable with the exception that at sixteen, weighing over two hundred pounds (and barely five feet tall), she'd not yet had her first period. The rash was something I'd seen before and I was able to have a teachable moment with the nurse practitioner about. Dorothy had a velvety dark discoloration in bands around her neck known as *acanthosis nigrans*. As opposed to other rashes that have an extrinsic cause, this finding is almost always associated with a systemic disease. Common in diabetics and sometimes simply connected with obesity, the finding is also associated with an underactive thyroid, otherwise known as hypothyroidism. So as I left the room, I suggested that she order a blood sugar test and a TSH test [9]—the hormone which is used as a marker for hypothyroidism.

The next day, as I leafed through the lab test results from the previous day, I came upon Dorothy's TSH result. I literally dropped the sheet! Her TSH level was over six hundred! Normally, the level is two to four. I'd never heard of a level this high. In effect, her pituitary gland was screaming, "Hey! We need more thyroxin!" Correcting her thyroid deficiency took several months of slow adjustment of her medication dose, but I called her two months later to ask her to get another TSH test done. When she picked up the phone, I thought I was talking to the wrong person. Contrasting the slow, flat, unemotional speech when we saw her with the rash two months before, this time she spoke rapidly, with modulated, excited phrases: "Oh yes, Dr. Johnston! I'll come in for that test tomorrow, and my grades are getting better, and I've lost twenty pounds and I had my first period!" In clipped succession, Dorothy told me as much as her follow up TSH would—she was getting better and her thyroid-starved metabolism was rebounding!

Other serendipitous findings emerge unexpectedly in doing a simple physical exam. Once I had a five-year-old patient who had ear troubles. I'll never forget the look his face when I pulled out a small piece of green plastic from his plugged ear. "Oh, that's a piece of Garfield! I thought that was lost!" he exclaimed. His mother only rolled her eyes.

Other unexpected physical findings take more explanation. Near the end of a busy day, even comical diversions can pop up. Sharon was a forty-five-year old waitress who hadn't been in for an exam for years and was having her first pelvic exam in a decade. She was somewhat overweight and anxious, as most women are, to "get this exam over with". As I stooped down to begin the exam, I noticed some small letters tattooed on her lower abdomen, which was out of her field of view because of increased abdominal girth over the last twenty years. I could make out the spelling of the name "Clem." It got me curious. "Tell me, Sharon. Who is Clem?" I blabbered without thinking. "H-h-how do you know about Clem?" she stuttered. So I composed myself, realizing what I was getting into. "Well…His name is tattooed down here." Her mood suddenly changed, probably relieved. "Oh my goodness! I haven't' seen that for years! Clem was my first boyfriend over thirty years ago." Fewer diversionary suggestions than usual were needed to distract Dorothy during what otherwise could have been a routine pelvic exam.

An occasional surprise finding can potentially result in dire consequences. In the flood of exams we have to do immediately prior to the school year are some that require a urine test. Although there are very rare times that something important is revealed, it's a "hoop that has to be jumped through." Jessica was a thirteen-year-old girl who wanted to try out for her middle school cheerleading squad. She was unsuccessful in producing a specimen on several trips to the bathroom and her mother, increasingly anxious to leave because she was late for work was getting impatient. Finally, she accompanied her daughter into the bathroom, and they emerged triumphantly a couple minutes later with the treasured sample. However, the plot thickened when my medical assistant reported that there was a *trace of blood* in the urine sample. Although I'd asked Jessica if she'd begun having her periods yet (and she said, "No"), I was suspicious she might have a urinary infection. The answer to questions about those symptoms was also "No." Mom was even more agitated when I told them I was going to do a microscopic exam on the urine. My puzzlement turned to horror when under the microscope, I found unmistakable *live sperm* in the sample! I didn't even tell the medical assistants. I went directly back into the room and talked with the mom. "I don't know quite how to ask this, but do you know if Jessica has had sexual contact with anyone? I found…" I hesitated, "sperm in her urine sample!" Mom's face immediately turned scarlet. "Oh my goodness, I'm sorry! I was so anxious to leave that I gave that sample myself. How could I have been so stupid!" By that time, Jessica had been there long enough that she could provide her own sample, and she passed the exam with flying colors. Even unexpected results are not always what they seem to be!

REFERRAL RARITIES

Imbedded in the remarkable diversity that has been a source of daily enjoyment for me as a family physician is the reality that I occasionally need help with an unusual or difficult diagnosis. Sometimes, the challenge of obtaining a referral for an indigent patient is daunting. In the first few years of my tenure at Broad Street, I would occasionally be faced with this response when calling a specialist to request a consult: "Uh, you're from that *free clinic* on the south side, aren't you? We can't take referrals like that." Or, a variation would be: "Our practice has decided to stop taking referrals of Medicaid patients." But as the clinic network developed credibility, referrals became easier and consultations more accessible.

Sometimes, consultants expressed their incredulity at the nature of the diseases referred to them. The case of Debra Wilkerson illustrates this well. Debra was twenty-two years old when she first visited our clinic. Her chief complaints were nearly diagnostic even before I walked into the examination room: tremors, weight loss, pounding heart, and lump in neck. As I examined her, it became obvious that she had not only classic hyperthyroidism but also the biggest goiter I'd ever seen. The thyroid gland in her neck was the size of a grapefruit and listening with my stethoscope over the enlarged gland, I could hear a distinct bruit—the audible sound of blood rushing through dilated vessels! She mentioned she'd also stopped having menstrual periods several months before, not uncommon with thyroid disease, but I still ordered a pregnancy test. Somewhat surprisingly, it was positive!

The next several months were a constant challenge to medically control her hyperthyroidism while ensuring the safety of her developing baby. Fortunately, Debra delivered a healthy girl near her due date, and we could turn full attention to treating her overactive thyroid gland. I arranged for a referral to my friend and nuclear medicine specialist, Dr. Hammons. He was a veteran radiologist with vast experience in treating hyperthyroidism with radioactive iodine, the definitive treatment in such cases. This therapy uses the affinity of the thyroid gland to take up iodine, making it possible to *nuke* it while minimizing exposure of the rest of the body to radiation.

Most letters from consultants after a referral start with such euphemistic phrases as, "Thank you for the opportunity to share in the treatment of this interesting patient...." or, "Ms. _____ is a pleasant __ year old patient who has had _____ for _____ years."

In Debra's case, I could almost see Dr. Hammons' incredulous wide-eyed expression when he wrote, "Debra Wilkerson has the most florid case of hyper-

THE POOR WITH ME

thyroidism I've ever seen, and her goiter is the biggest one I've ever treated!" This was no trivial statement since he'd been in practice over thirty years! The rest of his letter included an esoteric description of how he'd calculated the appropriate dose of radioactive iodine to treat a gland the size of hers, hopefully to maintain some degree of thyroid function afterward. He ended by saying that unfortunately, she had declined treatment! When I talked to him later, Dr. Hammons explained that when she'd heard that she couldn't hold her baby son for a couple of weeks after treatment because of potentially bad radiation effects on him, she decided she couldn't go through the iodine treatment and elected to continue taking her thyroid suppressive medication.

Visits after that time were sporadic, but she came in several times the following year after she'd run out of her medications. Her symptoms would always worsen, her weight would drop further, at one time bottoming out at ninety-seven pounds. Finally, when her tremulousness began to interfere with her daily life, she consented to treatment and at last, Dr. Hammons got the opportunity to treat "the biggest goiter he's ever seen." And then, Debra disappeared.

Two years later, I saw her name on the appointment list again. But when I walked into the exam room, I thought I'd made a mistake. This two-hundred-thirty-pound woman couldn't possibly be Debra Wilkerson! There was no goiter, and she was twice the size that she'd been two years before. Then I recognized the same person, transformed by what was now profound hypothyroidism! She had gone without any medication ever since her radioactive iodine treatment, assuming she'd been "cured". Instead, her treatment had killed off every remnant of her thyroid gland, and her body reflected the need for replacement thyroid hormone. Over ensuing years, Debra's weight bounced up and down like a yo-yo, driven by her inability to stay on her medication regularly. One time many years later when I saw Dr. Hammons at a medical staff meeting, he asked me about Debra. I told him, "You cured her goiter, but…."

Occasionally, the biggest challenge in a referral was determining what the actual problem was that required consultation. An exhausted mother called at the end of a summer vacation asking that her eight year old be referred for an *exorcism*! With little hope of finding a specialist able or willing to provide that service (much less finding an acceptable diagnostic code recognized by Medicaid!), I asked her to bring her troublesome son in for an exam. His ability to disassemble the examination table during the short time it took me to get into the room led rapidly to confirming a diagnosis of ADHD—attention deficit hyperactivity disorder. Within a few weeks of initiating treatment, not only was the exorcism referral unnecessary, but the threatening notes from the boy's teacher ceased and the mother was again sleeping at night.

Another category of referral is driven by its urgency—the true *emergency*. Ethel Warren was one of those rarities. She called the clinic early on a busy Friday afternoon. She'd never been seen at the Broad

Street Clinic before, but an alert triage nurse caught the sense of panic in her voice when she said, "My eye started hurting real bad this morning, and it's getting much worse so that I can't see very well out of it." Within half an hour, her son escorted her down the hall past where I was standing, writing in a chart. Out of the corner of my eye, I saw her shuffling along, holding an emesis basin in one hand and a scarf over her eye. Within a few seconds, I recognized what our ophthalmology professor had predicted might be a once-in-a-practice-lifetime diagnosis: acute angle closure glaucoma! Caused by a sudden blockage of the eye's drainage system, it brings a rapid buildup of pressure that is very painful and can lead quickly to permanent loss of vision.

Obtaining ophthalmologic referrals had always been one our most difficult consultations and the unfortunate timing of Ethel's emergency on a Friday afternoon boded ill for getting help. I knew that the county hospital had an ophthalmology resident on call nights and weekends and took a chance in calling in a page immediately. I was astounded to receive a return call within minutes from a friend who was in his second year of residency and was ecstatic to have the opportunity to treat an eye emergency himself!

There was one memorable instance when the referral process itself was diagnostic. Geraldine Oaks was one of my first patients with a perplexing heart condition. She'd had a loud heart murmur since adolescence but never had the opportunity to get a cardiology consultation. Although she had no history of rheumatic fever to cause the murmur or symptoms suggesting coronary artery disease, I was alarmed when she came in complaining of shortness of breath and occasional chest exertional pain. I felt compelled to get a consultation, so I called a cardiologist friend to make a referral. He was an amiable and experienced physician who was resonant with the unique needs of our patients; he made an appointment for Geraldine the next day.

I was gratified to receive a phone call from Dr. McGill the next day after he'd seen Mrs. Oaks. He reassured me that her murmur was *benign* and that her recent symptom changes were not cardiac related. "In fact," he said, "she certainly doesn't need a stress test! Do you know that she *walked* here from her home?" I gasped as I heard that because I knew his office was at least five miles north of downtown, and Geraldine's home was at least a mile south of the Broad Street Clinic— two miles *south* of downtown! Geraldine had passed a self-imposed stress test with an eight mile walk even before she got to Dr. McGill's office! Subconsciously, I chalked up another question I needed to ask before confirming a referral: "Do you have transportation to get there?"

THE BIG PAIN

A novel concept evolved in the '80s to assist medical providers in helping their patients to quantify and then follow the status of painful conditions. Known as the Wong-Baker smile scale, it allows patients to describe their perception of the severity of their pain using a visual and numerical rating and to assist care givers in comparing symptoms over time. A smiley face (zero on the numerical scale) indicates *no* pain. A crying face (ten on the numeric scale) indicates the worst imaginable pain. This tool was one of several innovations that the Broad Street Clinic adopted and made a part of each visit for those who experience pain.

But over the decades since its introduction, this useful tool has also given new life to a dark nemesis: the "drug seeking patient." Although certainly not unique to the inner city population, it has become an increasing

PHILIP E. JOHNSTON, MD

challenge in this patient demographic. Among many truly hurting patients are some who use exaggerated pain as a subterfuge to obtain prescription medications, sometimes to supply an addiction but often even worse, to be diverted for illicit use or sale. Although back pain, headaches, and anxiety are among the most common complaints drug-seeking patients use to legitimatize their request for medication, many have developed uncanny methods to impress primary care doctors that their complaints are legitimate.

Low back pain has been the most common complaint bringing in otherwise healthy young men to the Broad Street Clinic. Many of the jobs available to inner city patients are ones that predispose to mechanical back injuries: construction jobs, landscaping, factory, or warehouse work involving repetitive lifting, pushing, pulling, bending, and squatting. A very wise orthopedic professor I remember from my medical school days described very well how common back pain is: "If you are in primary care medical practice, ninety percent of your patients will eventually have back pain and the other ten percent are liars!" Unfortunately, many of these jobs, which lead to overuse syndromes including back pain, are also ones where disability leave is not tolerated; and patients seek any method to cover up the pain so that they can continue working, regardless of the consequences. Thus, the use and overuse of opiate analgesics is pervasive.

Earl was a twenty-seven-year old man who had been put on Vicodin after he fractured his ankle two years before his first visit to the Broad Street Clinic.

Although his ankle had long since healed, his job as a roofer (carrying heavy loads of shingles up ladders) made him predisposed to back strain. So, with the help of other providers, his opiate use had not only continued but escalated. By the time he showed up at our clinic, now with no insurance and during the winter when the roofing business had diminished, he wanted more opiates. When I confronted him with his normal exam and told him I would only give him doses of Vicodin for a programmed withdrawal, he was chagrined. Without realizing it, he had become strongly dependent on hydrocodone, the opiate constituent of Vicodin and faced several weeks of discomfort from withdrawal.

Bobby was a contrasting patient who rolled through the door of the clinic in a wheel chair. He claimed to have been on a bus passing through town when he began having severe flank pain, identical with the agony he reported having from passing a kidney stone three years before. He also had the grim history of a two-month stint in a hospital five years before after a violent auto accident followed by multiple surgical procedures on his back and legs. It was a compelling history to support a painful condition requiring a narcotic analgesic prescription. Concerned about his having complications from a kidney stone that wouldn't pass naturally, I asked Bobby to give us a urine specimen to look for blood.

The first clue I had that there might be some doubts about his condition was noticing that there were streaks of blood on his wheel chair wheels when he came back from the restroom. When I looked as his hand and saw a small fresh cut on his left little finger, he quickly said, "Oh, there must have been a little piece of glass stuck on the tire. I felt something sharp." Not surprisingly, the urine test *did* show considerable amount of blood.

He seemed satisfied when I told him that the signs suggested he was passing another kidney stone and that I'd like him to go to the hospital for an urgent ultrasound or CT scan. But he said that he needed to move on because he was traveling to visit a sister in a neighboring state, so we discussed which medication might be helpful in the interim. It was then that the proverbial red flags began to wave. Bobby told me, straight-faced, that he was allergic to most of the common narcotics (hydrocodone, oxycodone, codeine) and could only take Dilaudid, a hydromorphone product and one of the most potent and abusable opiate analgesics. Feeling that I was backed into a corner, I finally consented to giving him a prescription for twelve Dilaudid tablets and suggested that he see a urologist as soon as he got to his sister's home town.

I was disturbed to see a news report in the paper the next morning after he'd been arrested for forgery (changing my prescription to read one hundred twenty tablets) and for having three other prescriptions for Dilaudid from other providers that same day, one of which he was trying to sell to an undercover policeman.

Although Bobby may be the most egregious example of a drug seeker that I've faced in recent years, not a day goes by that I don't see another patient, often unwittingly, looking for inappropriate prescription relief of what (by their medical history) is a compelling problem. Since the daily stresses of life are often overwhelming in the inner city population, many patients seek relief of the resulting anxiety through the generous use of tranquilizers. A lack of supportive personal relationships also contributes to this reality. Generalized anxiety is a frequent result. Over years, I've developed the policy of treating acute, unexpected stress reactions (death of a loved one) or exposure to a severe fear-provoking situation (need to fly when phobic) with so-called minor tranquilizers such as clonazepam or alprazolam, the ever popular Xanax. Even this policy has proved vulnerable. Angela was a chronically anxious patient who often requested Xanax for family stresses. I usually complied with her requests until, after scanning her recent records, I discovered that the same maternal grandmother had "died" three times in the preceding year and a half!

We are fortunate to have experienced counselors working in the Broad Street Clinic who have developed considerable expertise in working with some of these patients to develop more effective coping skills and rely less on pharmacologic crutches. Yet, the challenge remains to give them appropriate medical help and to avoid iatrogenic (doctor-induced) drug dependence.

MATTERS OF FAITH

Since my own personal Christian faith had been such a powerful influence in my choice of career, in the early years of my practice at the Broad Street Clinic, I anticipated that many patients would resonate with that faith and that it would have a similarly transforming influence on their lives. My high hopes that this would be the case were buoyed as I walked around the clinic neighborhood on my lunch breaks. By my count, there were over sixty churches, many tiny, store-front locations, within a radius of six blocks of the clinic. Surely, there would be a strong tide of change physically, psychologically, *and* spiritually among my patients.

The reality became clear as I saw repeatedly that there was often a significant disconnection between patients' physical and spiritual lives. As is frequently the case in western cultures, there was a dualistic mentality about life. Everyday circumstances are part of a physical world, and matters of faith belonged in a spiritual world; the latter rarely intersected with life experienced on a daily basis, which included social disadvantages, poverty, and physical illness. Emotional illnesses seemed to be in some indeterminate position. This mentality was a philosophical inheritance, unrecognized and certainly unacknowledged, from the ancient Greek way of thinking. By contrast, in the many contacts my wife and I had with developing world cultures, particularly in Africa, the physical and spiritual worlds were unified; they thought monistically about life. The spiritual world was real and influenced the physical world significantly. As a result of their faith, many of my patients were confident that life hereafter would be better but they had despaired of their current everyday lives, physically and emotionally, changing for the better.

There is no question that as described in the Bible's New Testament, not everyone was healed of physical or emotional illnesses, but many were. Jesus fed thousands, but hunger still existed. Yet, I was (and still am) convinced that physical wholeness and spiritual wholeness are strongly connected. To be sure, one wholeness can exist without the other, but being spiritually whole can greatly enhance and influence the achievement of physical and emotional wholeness. Many of the patients I've seen over the years at the Broad Street Clinic illustrate this. Vera perhaps best represents that group because she experienced one of the most dramatic changes I've seen—physically and emotionally—as she found spiritual wholeness. Vera had the misfortune as so many of our patients do of being brought up in a fatherless family. By her teenage years, she desired attention from a male father figure so desperately that relationships with men became an obsession. I saw her for the first time when she had developed, for the second or third time, a case of pelvic inflammatory disease from a sexually acquired infection. In spite of these misfortunes, she was a bright young woman, had achieved a GED (graduate equivalent degree) and was hopeful of finding a legitimate career. Over five or ten years, I saw Vera repeatedly, for acute problems and sometimes, for stress related symptoms. Many times, we discussed the idea of what it was like to be truly *whole*—healed physically, emotionally, and spiritually. Although she'd never had any meaningful spiritual relationship at a personal or group level (she'd never attended a church), she was attracted enough to that idea that she often brought up the subject on her own. Finally, at the end of one visit when she was despairing at having lost another boyfriend relationship, I asked if I could pray for her. She readily consented, and we spent the last minutes of her visit praying together. That visit proved to be transformational. Although I didn't see her again for over a year, I received a letter from her a few months later, which is still in my file. She described having found faith herself and had connected with a church family that accepted her for who she was, nurturing her spiritual growth. She said that she'd finally experienced what we'd talked about at her last visit, genuine wholeness and with that, a new perspective on the future.

Have there been scores of examples like this to confirm my own faith? No, probably only a handful. Does that diminish my own faith or change my belief about the monistic overlap of the physical and spiritual world? Not at all. Is prayer a part of my therapeutic armamentarium? Certainly, especially on request! For many of my patients, their somewhat dualistic faith still serves as a sufficient promise for a better future. In the mean time, do I expect them all to be healed? Did Jesus heal everyone he had contact with? No, because the poor will always be with us, infected with the realities of an imperfect and broken world.

THE CHALLENGE
OF HIV/AIDS

Most physicians who went into practice in the '70s
remember vividly the first reports that came out in 1981
about clusters of young patients, mostly gay men on the
west coast, who were dying of mysterious infections.
As the disease was studied, it seemed to be one caused
by a new viral agent that attacked the body's immune
system, leaving it vulnerable to infections that had
rarely been seen in western medicine. It also became
clear that it was not exclusively a disease of gay men
and IV drug users. Other cases showed up in patients
who'd had blood transfusions and, eventually, average patients. The disease that we now know as HIV/
AIDS—acquired immune deficiency syndrome caused
by the human immunodeficiency virus—became a
world-wide pandemic.

It took almost a decade before this virus made its
presence known at the Broad Street Clinic. In typical fashion, it crept in the back door. In the last half
of the '80s, our clinics became one of the state centers

for doing immigration physicals. At first, these were superficial physical exams combined with required blood tests: a test for syphilis and an HIV test. Only one in a hundred or more were positive for the first five years—all for syphilis. Then, we had our first positive HIV test. I'd not seen this patient for her physical, but I had the responsibility of explaining the positive HIV test to her. She was a twenty-seven-year-old Hispanic immigrant from Mexico. She was exquisitely beautiful, but she spoke only broken English. Through an interpreter, I told her about the positive test. It was as though I'd hit her on the head with a club; she sank down in her chair, stunned and silent. Then, the tears started. She stammered in English, "This means, I will...die"? In those early years, HIV infection almost always was a death sentence. The anti-viral medications we have now to prolong HIV infected patients' lives almost indefinitely didn't exist then. I put a comforting arm around her shoulders and said, "Not necessarily. There are new studies being done all the time." There were frankly very few support programs in those early days, especially for non-English speakers. What I had to offer her was mostly sympathy and some vaguely encouraging words. "Why did this happen to me?" she asked. "I've been good...." I ended that encounter depressed with little to offer her.

Ann could hardly have been a more contrasting patient. She'd been my patient for years, and at fifty-five was still unmarried, but she had a boyfriend. She was overweight, had diabetes, and was mildly mentally handicapped. She could write her name, but she'd never mastered the skill of reading. I would have considered her at very low risk for HIV, but ironically at one visit, she asked, "Dr. Johnston, I'd like t' have one of them there AIDS tests." At first, I was a bit surprised and said, "Ann, why do you want us to do that?" After some thought, Ann said simply, "I want it 'cause I saw my boyfriend comin' out of a men's room with a man who had long hair." I was still doubtful but did the test. Imagine my shock when Ann was the second woman I'd seen with a positive test! Fortunately, her CD4 count was still high and with the help of an infectious disease expert, she survived many more years. She ended the relationship, at my urging, with her boyfriend.

Although there were several more HIV/AIDS incidents over the years, a third patient will forever stay in my memory because of the ethical and moral problem it presented. Virtually every primary care doctor is sometimes faced with the dilemma of how to respond to family and friends who request care. There are some unavoidable challenges with objectivity and confidentiality that always arise in relationships like that. However, there are times when both the need and the relationship justify sharing a physician's skills, even knowing the risks involved. A long time family friend called me to ask if I'd see a friend of her son's. He was destitute and had just moved to the Midwest from the West Coast. She said he'd had a cough for a month that he couldn't shake and wondered if I'd take a look at him. Although, as always, some warning bells went off in the distance, I consented and made Evan an appointment.

A few days later at his appointment, most of my fears were allayed when I walked into the examination room. Evan was a delightful young man of twenty-nine, articulate, well-dressed, and pleasant to talk with. He looked perfectly healthy. I didn't hear him cough once. As we talked, it appeared he'd moved to our community because a job had opened up with a local theater that exactly fit his training and experience. He was excited to be here to accept this new career opportunity. By his report, he'd been healthy, rarely had needed to see a doctor and had only been bothered by this *nagging cough* for a few weeks. To do the exam, I asked him to take his shirt off; surprisingly, he seemed a bit reluctant, but complied. His head and neck exam seemed normal, but when I walked around to his back to listen to his lungs, I was horrified to see dozens of purplish blotches covering his skin. Although I'd only seen pictures of Kaposi's Sarcoma, the alarm of recognition was jangling wildly. I hoped I could mask my anxiety as I listened to his chest. There were only a few nonspecific rattles, but my heart was racing. "Evan," I said as I walked around in front of him, "how long have you had those...spots...on your back?" He didn't blink an eye when he said, "Oh those blue things? They've been there for over a year." I cleared my throat nervously. Finally I said, "Have you ever had a test for HIV?" Again without hesitancy he said, "Oh yes, just a few months before I came out here, and it was negative." I then explained my concerns about his skin lesions, that they were consistent with a defining infection of AIDS and that I'd like to do an HIV test today. Then,

Evan began to be evasive. "I can't afford it…and I had one just a few months ago…and I feel fine." Finally, thinking of my friend, I said I would pay for it and he consented to get the test done. I left the room to see the next patient and told the medical assistants that they were to draw an HIV antibody test on Evan. A few minutes later, I came out of the next room to find that Evan had left and refused to have the test done! That left me with the dilemma of what to do next. Although I was suspicious that he had AIDS (with lesions typical of Kaposi Sarcoma), I didn't really have proof of a positive blood test. Although I had no idea what kind of relationship he had with my friend's son, I was apprehensive about the possibilities. Did I have the right to inform my friend's son?

Over the next three weeks, I made innumerable calls to my friend's son's house. Evan was not home— repeatedly. I left messages for him to call, but there was no return. I even called the theater where he worked. Still, I couldn't establish contact. Finally, I called the theater and said, "I'll wait until you find Evan. It's an emergency that I talk with him." After interminable minutes, Evan picked up the phone. "Evan," I said, "this is Dr. Johnston. I'm disappointed you didn't get that test. We *must* do it, with no excuses this time!" Again, there was a long pause, followed by, in a peculiarly apt theatrical style, a whisper, "Okay, I'll do it".

A few days later, I got Evan's HIV results back. It was strongly *positive*. The week after that, he consulted an infectious disease specialist; his CD4 count was alarmingly low at six. Sometime later, I had a chance to talk with my friend's son about Evan. It turned out that he was staying there with no intimate relationship involved other than a place to stay. Ironically, he surmised why I was calling. "I knew it had to be something like that; no doctor would call that many times about a missed appointment!" After six months, I saw Evan's obituary in the newspaper.

THE POOR WITH YOU

Poverty in the United States is an embarrassing blight on the landscape of the richest country on earth. The stories you've read describe the lives of a tiny population of medical patients who have endured some of the vicissitudes of poverty while all around them, they see the fleeting images of extravagant wealth.

To be sure, poverty that we see in the U.S. is mild in comparison to many other countries. Nowhere in the U.S. will you find the equivalent of the Kibera slum in Nairobi, Kenya. That city within a city, where my wife and I have visited several times, is home for over a million people whose very lives, not to mention homes, meals, clothing, teeter in precarious balance every day. You won't find sprawling refugee camps such as those in northern Uganda where hundreds of thousands of families live, depending every day on the benevolence of a sometimes antagonistic host country and the desperate outreach of a variety of charitable NGOs for their survival.

Those of us who are blessed with a menu of options to choose from move comfortably through daily lives where want is usually for something we don't truly need. Often we develop a practiced avoidance to those around us who live in poverty. It is easy to opt for a path on a downtown sidewalk to avoid confrontation with a street panhandler. It becomes a convenient necessity for us to avert our eyes from a homeless man advertising "Will work for food" when stopped at a traffic light. A career in medical care for impoverished inner city dwellers is a relatively easy way to reach out to those with health needs who can't afford the financial demands of traditional health care. The Broad Street Clinic and its sister clinics offer a sliding fee scale that allows respectable entry into an otherwise inaccessible system. Those of you who have read the stories told in previous chapters and who have similar connections with the medical community can resonate with some of the vignettes, laugh occasionally, and struggle with the emotions of helplessness and frustration that often arise.

But how do those of us who are relatively insulated from the harsh realities of poverty in general and the medical needs of neglected populations specifically find a way to build bridges in helping those who are less fortunate living in or near our communities? A detailed solution to this pervasive problem is far beyond the scope of this book and would be a naïve goal at best! But let me offer some suggestions about easily available ways to begin to make first steps.

In some communities where the population can't support an independent Federally Qualified Health Clinic (FQHC) system for uninsured patients, there are free clinics staffed by volunteer medical personnel. Practicing physicians in the community band together, volunteering their time to serve. Nurses, pharmacists, medical assistants, therapists, and other medical professionals also can contribute their skills and experiences in such a setting. Sometimes, inner city missions and large inner city churches have their own clinics that offer care for the neediest in a community, also relying on volunteer help. Identifying those opportunities can serve as a starting point to be involved in addressing the day-to-day medical needs of those living in poverty. The prospect of national Healthcare Reform may provide access to care for a much broader population. Until then, at both a local and an international level, this website can provide advice about opportunities: www.healthcarevolunteer.com.

Much poverty in our country is accompanied by diminished literacy. Families grow up together not valuing written stories, rarely occupying leisure time with anything but television and seldom enjoying the relationships that grow from reading together. The Broad Street Clinic has, for many years, participated in a program called "Reach Out and Read." (You may visit www.reachoutandread.org for more details.) Books for appropriate reading levels are offered free of charge to children with their parent; most importantly, reading is modeled by having volunteers read to children awaiting appointments in our waiting rooms. Often, a parent seeing this mentoring process for the first time will realize, "I could do that…" Rarely have young mothers experienced the joy of reading with their own parents, so the novelty of reading with their own children is a revelation.

Many inner city schools are desperate for the help that student tutors can offer the children whose families are dysfunctional or absent. The resulting educational delays can be helped immensely by the one-on-one relationship that a couple hours per week with a tutor in reading or math provides. A simple phone call to the school administration office can open the door. On a national level, there are multitudes of mentoring possibilities. The web site, www.mentoring.org, is an excellent starting point and resource for interested volunteers.

Natural disasters both within and outside of the United States often have the greatest effect on those who live with the reality of poverty. Hurricanes, floods, earthquakes are not respecters of social class or financial status, but memories of disasters such as Hurricane Katrina and the earthquake in Haiti dramatically illustrate how uniquely vulnerable those who live in poverty are. Many who have joined the organized teams providing help after these calamities have had life-transforming experiences themselves.

Several agencies with deep Christian roots such as Habitat for Humanity and Samaritan's Purse provide opportunities to serve in practical ways for relief of the daily needs of those in poverty. Habitat for Humanity (www.habitat.org) provides access for those who can volunteer brief or longer periods of time both locally and abroad to build homes for the most needy in areas where options are limited. Samaritan's Purse (www.

samaritanspurse.org) also has a broad palette of opportunities available utilizing many areas of training in hundreds of locations worldwide. Another great website for students who wish to know more about poverty is the thinkquest.org. (Go to http://thinkquest.org/pls/html/think.library and query *poverty*.) It has a large listing of agencies that are internationally involved in poverty relief.

Not many feel called to invest a lifetime in a culture of poverty. But all of us are strengthened by recognizing the *poor with us* and can serve as agents of change by reaching out to those in desperate need.

EPILOGUE:
WHY ARE YOU HERE?

Over the forty years I've spent in medical practice in the inner city, hundreds of medical students and residents have spent time with me, learning ambulatory care. Almost predictably after a week or two, every student would, with a somewhat glazed look in their eyes, venture the question, "Why are you here, doing what you're doing?" Or, "How can you keep doing this?" After a week in inner city medicine, facing the constant challenges of difficult patients, perpetual financial constraints—diagnostic tests, therapeutic options, referrals—these young physicians began to realize the stark differences between what they'd been trained to do in the medical center or hospital setting and the reality of the inner city. In the early days, over eighty percent of our patients had no insurance and no disposable income to devote to health care. Preventive care was a foreign concept. Chronic diseases such as high blood pressure, diabetes, high cholesterol, obesity, and premature atherosclerotic heart disease were rampant. The proportion of adults who smoked was over sixty percent, twice the national average. Emotional problems were pervasive; it seemed like everyone was anxious or depressed—or both. We saw acute illnesses such as measles and mumps that had disappeared for the most part in the suburban populations. For many students, the challenges of practicing medicine in this setting seemed overwhelming.

To adequately answer the *why* questions, I often went back to the beginning of my journey into medicine. Although I was the first person in my extended family going back many generations to train for medicine as a career, I'd always been fascinated by life science. What makes living things work? How does it all fit together? More importantly, how does a person apply their strong Christian faith in the role of a physician? School always came easy for me, so I wasn't daunted by the prospects of interminable training years. My parents nurtured my curiosity and affirmed my ambition to pursue a medical career. I was fascinated by the diversity of specialties in medicine but the then fledgling field of family medicine offered both the tremendous diversity I enjoyed as well as the prospect of long lasting relationships with patients that I found fulfilling.

Marriage during medical school was a good way to hone skills in frugality that had been an important part of both my wife's and my growing up years. Together, we planned for the future and determined very early that *bigger and better* and *more and more* were not important values for us. We were content to live with little, paying for medical school expenses as we went along from my wife's meager teacher salary. Our faith had always been the most important priority in our lives, and all these early decisions were shaped by those values. Late in my junior year, the opportunity to spend the precious quarter off prior to my senior year doing a three-month externship at a mission hospital in South Africa arose. We had hardly enough money to visit my wife's parents seven hundred miles away, but through the help of generous friends and a scholarship, our way was paid.

Those three months were transforming. We saw a part of the world we'd only imagined before: we witnessed poverty on a scale we could scarcely conceive, and most crucially, saw medical needs of mind-bending extent. The three months were filled with countless new experiences—for me medically and for my wife educationally as she taught in a tiny school on the compound in rural Zululand. I went from being a naive mid-western junior medical student to being an assistant in life-saving surgeries, doing multiple obstetrical deliveries and C-sections, treating tetanus, managing the complications of countless cases of TB, and other *exotic* infections among innumerable other challenges. As world events unfolded, we also listened to the first moon landing on short wave radio. At that time, Apartheid in South Africa was so pervasive that television was illegal because of the threat of having more inclusive western racial policies portrayed to their population!

After our whirlwind of experiences for three months, we were ready to return to Africa for our future. But as my senior year of training proceeded and I began to see the medical needs and the developing *culture of poverty* in *our* inner cities [10], I realized that my calling to help the poor and medically underserved could take place in my own back yard! I began to moonlight in some of the burgeoning number of neighborhood health centers in our city and soon recognized that this indeed was where my future practice would be.

A glimpse at the evolution of—and need for—these inner city health care facilities enhances background for the stories. In most large American cities, a gradual migration from the inner cities to the suburbs began in the '50s, accelerated in the '60s, and became a tsunami in the '70s. Accompanying this movement was the invasion of the big cities by the expanding interstate highway system. As the "outer belts" were connected to downtown "inner belt" interstates, old neighborhoods that had evolved into close-knit communities over decades were transected and sliced up by eminent domain and the higher priority of access to downtown jobs by the now suburban commuters. Typically, physicians who had practiced in these neighborhoods followed the migration with their practices. Or, older general practitioners retired rather than face the disruption of moving their practices. Long standing doctor–patient relationships ended and thousands of inner city residents who, for various reasons, couldn't follow the migration, found themselves suddenly without care and without easy access to medical services. More viable neighborhood groups banded together, sometimes purchasing old churches, banks, or other abandoned facilities. These were then renovated to provide an often primitive setting for health care.

Volunteer providers—usually resident physicians—were then recruited to provide spotty health care. In some of these early clinics where I worked, the examination rooms were merely curtained off spaces where privacy was minimal and to do a pelvic exam, I'd often bump into someone in an adjacent room through the curtain when I bent over!

A few systems had the good fortune to have innovative and imaginative young professionals to spearhead the development of more sophisticated and permanent organizations. A good friend of mine, a couple years ahead of me in training, was such an entrepreneur. A fellow family physician, he had the vision to start a single health center in the late '60s which blossomed into three clinics by the early '70s staffed by salaried, full-time physicians. The defining characteristic of this clinic system was *accessibility*—they were located in the neighborhoods where the patients lived. As well, charges were based on a sliding fee scale. When a patient entered the system, they had a financial interview, and their fee was based on that income.

As I finished my residency, I was painfully aware that many of my colleagues who had gone into traditional private practice were rapidly trapped by the compelling time demands and, more insidiously, by the *work-more-to-earn-more* temptation. Marriages faltered; families were disrupted. The cost of financial success was failure in areas my wife and I valued most. At the time I finished my residency, we had two young children and I wanted to assure that I could invest predictable time in their lives without the threat of being married to my practice instead of my wife. A salaried position for a family physician was almost unheard of in the early '70s, but this new health center system offered that with a somewhat predictable nine to five schedule. Best of all, it also allowed me to practice in a setting where I felt truly called and could apply the caring and compassion consistent with my Christian faith. I was even provided the advantage of being able to spend the majority of my practice time during the last year of my residency in the facility on Broad Street, an authentic trial run to assure that this was the type of practice for me. The affirmation of many patients like Lottie Gray and countless others, some of whose stories I've told confirmed that this was to be *my* place.

Did the students who asked me those questions understand this story? Perhaps only a few truly resonated with both my reasoning and the values that supported it. But several students who had that initial exposure returned to practice there at future times. And most of them respected the role, even though it would not be their choice of practice location. At later times as I met those students again after they'd been in practice elsewhere, a common question would follow—and many other friends and fellow physicians ask the same question, "Are you staying busy?" My answer was usually the same: "I have one of the few types of medical practice with a literally *Biblical* promise that I'll always be busy." This response was based on a vignette in the life of Jesus as recorded by the gospel writer Matthew. As he approached the end of his short life on Earth, Jesus was in the company of his disciples when an admiring woman demonstrated her deep love and respect for him by pouring a lavish amount of expensive perfume on his head. As they questioned the propriety of this action, some disciples objected, implying that she could have used this offering more appropriately by giving it to the poor. Jesus answered in part justifying her action because of his impending departure, "What she has done is a good thing…but *the poor you will always have with you…*"

ENDNOTES

1   Restore a normal heart rhythm with an electrical shock.

2   Wolf-Parkinson-White Syndrome, requiring surgery or a sophisticated electrical short circuiting procedure to correct it.

3   A technique of speaking after laryngectomy using swallowed air and vocalizing by "belching" words.

4   Coughing up blood.

5   Probably so-called "Pseudo-pseudo hypoparathyroidism".

6   From a lecture by Dale S. Benson, MD on poverty given to the St. Vincent Hospital Family Medicine residency in 1998.

7   A rating system using numbers 1-10 to record a baby's relative health a minute after birth.

8   The special way of staining the TB germ to iden-
    tify it under the microscope.

9   TSH is the abbreviation for thyroid stimulat-
    ing hormone, the factor produced by the "mas-
    ter gland", the pituitary gland in the head which
    stimulates the thyroid to make more of the thy-
    roid hormone, thyroxin.

10 An article that appeared in Scientific American
    about the "Culture of Poverty" describing the
    way multiple generations of families were slowly
    trapped in inner-city poverty by loss of fam-
    ily cohesion, absent fathers, diminished value
    of education, a sense of entitlement and pessi-
    mism about the future had a formative influence
    on me.

CPSIA information can be obtained at www.ICGtesting.com
Printed in the USA
LVOW08s1553300914

406573LV00016B/853/P